Get a Better Job

Teach® Yourself

Get a Better Job
Rod Ashley

For UK order enquiries: please contact Bookpoint Ltd,
130 Milton Park, Abingdon, Oxon OX14 4SB.
Telephone: +44 (0) 1235 827720. Fax: +44 (0) 1235 400454.
Lines are open 09.00–17.00, Monday to Saturday, with a 24-hour
message answering service. Details about our titles and how to
order are available at www.teachyourself.com

Long renowned as the authoritative source for self-guided
learning – with more than 50 million copies sold worldwide –
the **Teach Yourself** series includes over 500 titles in the fields of
languages, crafts, hobbies, business, computing and education.

British Library Cataloguing in Publication Data: a catalogue record
for this title is available from the British Library.

This edition published 2010.

Previously published as *Getting a Better Job*

The **Teach Yourself** name is a registered trade mark of
Hodder Headline.

Typeset by MPS Limited, a Macmillan Company.

Printed in Great Britain for Hodder Education, an Hachette UK
Company, 338 Euston Road, London NW1 3BH, by CPI Cox &
Wyman, Reading, Berkshire RG1 8EX.

The publisher has used its best endeavours to ensure that the URLs
for external websites referred to in this book are correct and active
at the time of going to press. However, the publisher and the
author have no responsibility for the websites and can make no
guarantee that a site will remain live or that the content will remain
relevant, decent or appropriate.

Hachette UK's policy is to use papers that are natural, renewable
and recyclable products and made from wood grown in sustainable
forests. The logging and manufacturing processes are expected to
conform to the environmental regulations of the country of origin.

Impression number   10 9 8 7 6 5 4 3 2 1

Year   2014 2013 2012 2011 2010

Front cover: © Lisa F. Young – Fotolia.com

Back cover: © Jakub Semeniuk/iStockphoto.com, © Royalty-
Free/Corbis, © agencyby/iStockphoto.com, © Andy Cook/
iStockphoto.com, © Christopher Ewing/iStockphoto.com,
© zebicho – Fotolia.com, © Geoffrey Holman/iStockphoto.com,
© Photodisc/Getty Images, © James C. Pruitt/iStockphoto.com,
© Mohamed Saber – Fotolia.com

Contents

Meet the author

Rod Ashley owns Ashley Consult (www.ashley-consult.co.uk), which incorporates Ashley Associates and CATS. It provides consultancy and training services to a wide range of clients, such as local authorities, the BBC, universities, private companies, the European Commission and the Welsh Assembly Government.

Rod's first job was as a school teacher, before becoming a college lecturer and manager. Transferring to a university, he also became involved in staff development and moved into full-time consultancy in 1997. He has led several national organizations in skills and people development, and holds Expert status with the European Commission. He has written extensively: this is Rod's 25th book with major publishers in 25 years of writing – an unexpected achievement of which he is proud. An elected Fellow of several major bodies, including the Royal Society of Arts and a former Council Member of the BBC, Rod also cherishes a certificate in pretzel-making from a Pennsylvanian bakery.

Outside work, Rod enjoys travel, classic cars and is slowly trying to master digital photography. He avoids DIY wherever possible. Married to Moira and with two grown-up daughters, Rod admires them all for their own many achievements.

Future ambitions? Piloting a helicopter, owning a reliable classic car, visiting New Zealand, keeping chickens and bees and, in time, an active, healthy retirement.

Only got a minute?

We all know that the era of 'a job for life' has gone.
Flexible working practices, multi-tasking,
interdisciplinary teams, home-working, outsourcing
... all of these have changed the secure world of
work which many of us grew up with and expected
to continue. Additionally, the nature of many jobs
themselves has changed. Indeed, in some cases,
the work our young people in school will do when they
leave has not yet been invented. Just as those of us
who started work before the PC revolution in the early
1980s could not have predicted the development of 'IT
architects' or 'imagineers', so it is difficult to envisage
the impact of technological changes on work and
society in the future.

To survive and prosper in the new world
of work requires self-confidence, self-knowledge,
a proactive approach to up-skilling yourself and
an acceptance that skills and a flexible mindset go

hand in hand with subject knowledge or technical expertise.

This book will encourage you to reflect on why and how work is changing, on what you know about your current employment sector and, most importantly, on what you know about yourself. Carefully devised toolkits enable you to reflect systematically, to identify your strengths and weaknesses and to plan for the future. After reading this book you will feel more secure in your own knowledge and ability to grasp your own working future more confidently.

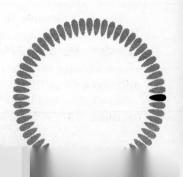

5 Only got five minutes?

We have all heard that phrase 'a job for life'. What's more, we have all heard that this reassuring concept has gone. But what, exactly, has replaced it? The current, fast-changing economic climate shows us that, across the world, many people are adopting more flexible working practices, they are involved in multi-tasking and work in interdisciplinary teams. Many people now work fully or partly from home – not the old piecemeal assembly work of the early industrial revolution in Europe, but more flexible IT-based home working – coming into a central office perhaps only periodically. Many employers outsource aspects of non-core work to self-employed, portfolio workers who can bring expertise to projects or initiatives on a 'just-in-time' basis and do not carry the direct overheads of employed staff.

All these examples illustrate the change from the secure world of work which many of us grew up with and have expected to continue. Additionally, the nature of many jobs themselves has changed. Indeed, in some cases, the work our young people in school will do has not yet been invented. Just as those of us who started work before the PC revolution in the early 1980s could not have predicted the development of 'IT architects' or 'imagineers', so it is difficult to envisage the impact of technological changes on work and society in the future.

This creates a very different working environment. Offices have moved beyond the open-plan layout – they may now be virtual offices because some people work from home. For many, the prospect of working partly from home may seem attractive – avoiding stressful commuting and petty office politics. Yet, for others, the prospect is unattractive – you need strong time-management skills and the self-discipline to avoid becoming distracted by family activities, surfing the internet or a sunny garden.

In general, to survive and prosper in this new world of work requires self-confidence, self-knowledge and an acceptance that skills and a flexible mindset go hand in hand with subject knowledge or technical expertise. The years of racking up extensive experience in a specific field may be less important now than the ability to grasp and run with new ideas, to be a self-starter, or to work with colleagues asynchronously. Certainly, it places a greater focus on interpersonal skills and how to work with people most effectively through a variety of media and settings.

Throughout this book, a range of case studies from three different employment sectors illustrate the tussle people may have with these decisions – their fears, indecision and frustration, as well as a need to satisfy their inner potential. You will be able to match the decisions you are making against three fictional characters. They all resolve their issues – this book provides you with the toolkit and encouragement to do the same.

Get a Better Job: Teach Yourself will encourage you to reflect on why and how work is changing, on what you know about your current employment sector and, most importantly, on what you know about yourself. Carefully selected toolkits enable you to reflect systematically on these issues, to identify your strengths and weaknesses and to plan for the future. After reading this book you will feel more secure in your own knowledge and ability to grasp the future more confidently. Even if traditional job security is diminishing, you will feel more secure personally in handling your own working future.

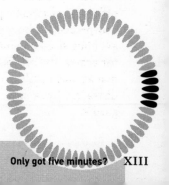

Preface

What this book aims to do

Never has the nature of work changed so quickly – a global economy and the power of electronic communication means that news travels immediately. When economic events in the US or Asia happen, they are beamed to us straight away. Bad news about jobs or economic trends has no hiding place. But good news also travels quickly so that we can see trends in recovery and emerging opportunities. This allows individuals to be prepared for the changing jobs market – and this book will show you a range of invaluable tools to use to stay ahead of the game.

The aims of this book are to explore the various factors which have caused the changes in ideas about work and in attitudes to work. It will also encourage you to explore how you can prepare yourself for these changes and gain the greatest satisfaction from your work.

That's a tall order for any book. But it won't just be me as author trying to achieve that change. In order to gain most value from this book, you, as reader, will need to enter into the 'activities' in a positive frame of mind. You will need to ask yourself some searching and fundamental questions. You may need to discuss various issues with a partner, close friends or colleagues. You will need to live with the answers you provide, but also actively seek to enhance those skills and qualities where you can do so.

In essence the book adopts the well-known strategic management plan of:

- ▶ *Where are you now?*
- ▶ *Where do you want to be?*
- ▶ *How are you going to get there?*

Understanding the structure of the book

This book will guide you through that helpful process in clear stages, so you should aim to read through it in the order printed. Whilst there are sections which you can use as reference sources in the future (e.g. Chapter 8: Where are you going next?), you will gain the greatest benefit by reading the book in sequence and giving yourself time to reflect on some of the issues. By all means return to sections at a later time – to re-read them or to update your personal response to the issues raised.

In essence, following the list of contents, the chapters in this book will help you to help yourself by:

▶ *outlining the changing patterns of employment*
▶ *explaining the rationale for such changes*
▶ *encouraging you to get to know yourself as a worker and a person*
▶ *establishing what motivates you*
▶ *understanding what you have to offer*
▶ *developing your employability skills*
▶ *assessing your attitude to life*
▶ *establishing where you are going next*
▶ *devising your personal action plan and*
▶ *accessing some additional support and sources of further information.*

When you have finished reading this book, you should understand more about the nature of work today and also more about yourself. A number of pointers will have been offered to you but it is ultimately up to you to decide what to do about them. The book will not preach and will not suggest ideas or ways of life you should follow. It aims simply to open your eyes (and other senses) to these opportunities so that you can make your decision based upon self-knowledge and understanding.

Take comfort from what you learn are your strengths, have the courage to develop your weaknesses and learn to recognize where you have control over your life and work.

At the back of the publication you will find a list of other sources of helpful support and information. If you are particularly interested in, for example, theories of motivation, you will find a booklist to guide you in exploring these issues in greater depth.

If the book that follows meets those aims, I extend my thanks to family, friends and colleagues for their help and advice along life's way. In particular, over the last fifteen years I have been very fortunate in my own career to work in different contexts with three exceptional and inspiring colleagues – Kath Durbin, Marie Fleming and Dr Cheryl Morgan. In her own unique way, each has brought great vision, energy and personal attributes to our shared work, enriched my own career and enhanced the aspirations and life opportunities of many people.

I celebrate the many and varied achievements of my daughters Fiona and Louise, both of whom have already made significant marks in their respective professions and have also grown into globally confident young women. Above all, I extend my gratitude to my wife, Moira, for reading drafts of the manuscript, making valuable comments and suggestions and – more importantly and with my love – for encouraging me to identify and articulate my own employability skills when the solid ground of employment proved illusory many years ago.

To balance the all-female list above, this book is dedicated to the memory and abiding influence of my late father, Major 'Rufus' Ashley BEM, TD, who met head-on the challenges of life with bravery, dignity, wisdom and good humour; and to my newborn, first grandson, Louis Rhys Chaillier-Zeiler.

All those named above are my own 'sad captains'. In one of the activities in Chapter 2 of this book I hope that you can identify your own influences.

Rod Ashley, Swansea 2010

Acknowledgements

From: *JOBSHIFT: How to Prosper in a Workplace Without Jobs* by William Bridges, published by Nicholas Brealey Publishing.

From: *The Poetry of Robert Frost* edited by Edward Connery Lathem, published by Jonathan Cape, together with acknowledgements to The Estate of Robert Frost.

From: *Team Roles at Work* by R. Meredith Belbin, published by Butterworth-Heinemann, 1993. Permission granted by Belbin.com, Cambridge, UK.

My thanks also to the following people: Bob Brennan of Bob Brennan Associates, Sheffield; Ronnie Davidson of The Career Studio, Cupar, Fife; and Alison Frecknall, my publisher at Hodder, for her assistance, enthusiasm and trust in me for this third book with her.

1

Moving from employment to employability

In this chapter you will learn:
- *about the changing nature of work*
- *what we mean by the term 'employability'*
- *about three individuals whose career choices we will follow*
- *why it is important to share your responses with others*

Understanding how these changes are affecting you

This book starts with two premises: firstly, that the traditional
job pattern has gone and secondly, that the traditional covenant
between employer and employee has also gone – both of them
for good. The expectations of our parents for employment (theirs
and ours) have disappeared. That does not mean to say that there
will be *un*employment, although inevitably there will be some.
Indeed, current figures reflect the economic recession. Rather,
it means that whilst there will be fewer jobs, there will still be
work. That may appear to be something of a conundrum, so let's
start to spell it out.

> Instead of the traditional employer/employee covenant to which
> we have all grown accustomed, workers will need to take on a
> different attitude or 'mindset' towards the concept of work.

For many generations, there has been the passive expectation of becoming an employee – of devoting x hours a week and y years to a particular employer in return for z salary and a sense of security. Now, there must be much more active selling of the skills, experience and qualities which each individual can offer.

Understanding the future of work

Back in February 1998, the Government's Green Paper about the future of learning (to equip people with the vital knowledge and skills for a new century) stated that:

> **The information and knowledge-based revolution of the twenty-first century will be built upon ... investment in the intellect and creativity of people.**
>
> *The Learning Age*, Introduction, Section 1.4. February 1998

> **Individuals should invest in their own learning to improve their employability, professional competence, and earning potential or for leisure.**
>
> ibid., Chapter 2, 2.5. February 1998

Note that the government identified 'employability' as a key issue as we all became knowledge workers in the twenty-first century. More recent UK government policies extended this theme, encouraging everyone to update their skills and knowledge. Indeed, the Welsh Assembly Government document *A Winning Wales* (January 2002) aimed for:

> **A dynamic, inclusive and sustainable economy based on successful, innovative businesses with highly-skilled, well-motivated people.**

However, trying to achieve this, whether in Wales or across the UK, is in the context of a rapidly-changing backdrop.

INVESTING IN OUR FUTURE

Britain can only succeed in a rapidly-changing world if we develop the skills of our people to the fullest possible extent ... and apply both knowledge and skills to create an innovative and competitive economy.

UK Department for Innovation, Universities and Skills
(DIUS) mission statement, 2007

Likewise, the UK Commission for Employment and Skills re-states the need for creativity in skills strategies:

We want to see more people in the workforce with more of the right skills. That's easy to say, and it's a goal shared by employers, politicians and the general public alike. Putting strategies in place which will achieve this goal is much more difficult, but it's essential if the UK is to succeed, both as an economically competitive, and socially inclusive, nation.

Chris Humphries CBE, Chief Executive of the UK
Commission for Employment and Skills, August 2008

Government figures confirm that the last decade or so has seen fundamental changes to the UK employment scene. There is an increase in the number of part-time workers (now totalling 28% of all workers), of short-term contracts and of people retiring or being retired early. In some cases, the percentage of people taking early retirement through ill-health is staggeringly high. For example, according to the Pensions Policy Institute (2005) in the UK public sector, 68% of fire-fighters, 49% of police, 39% of local government staff, 25% of teachers, 23% of NHS staff, 22% of civil servants and 6% of the armed service retire before their official retirement age. By contrast, under 20% of private sector workers retire through ill-health early. Indeed all workers' tax continues to fund public sector pensions. At the same time, the proportion of people feeling secure about their job (particularly in the private sector) fell from 96% in 1990 to 43% in 1996.

In summary:

- ▶ *there is a reduction in the level of full-time male employment*
- ▶ *there is an increase in the level of female employment (but not necessarily full-time or permanent)*
- ▶ *there are fundamental changes in working patterns, and*
- ▶ *the shift in employment has been away from large employers to small and medium enterprises (SMEs).*

Let's take a brief journey through history to examine the changing nature of work from the earliest time to today to see what has brought about these changes affecting us now.

PROGRESSING FROM STONE-AGE CLUB TO GOLD WATCH

The Stone Age
There were clearly distinct gender differences. A man's task was to provide for his family by meeting their basic survival needs – food, clean water, providing shelter and warmth. Women's task was to rear children and to cook food brought home by men.

The Iron Age and Bronze Ages
The role of men became more sophisticated as they designed and created more intricate weapons with which to slay both animals and human aggressors. They also became skilled in being able to forge small pieces of precious metal – coins – to exchange for other items.

The Middle Ages
The beginnings of international trade and specialization in work started (e.g. a shoe-maker was able to sell shoes to villages or exchange these for goods/services such as repair to the wheel of his cart). The concept of division of labour and of a service having a cash value had started.

The Elizabethan Age
This was the 'Age of Discovery', trade and shops. The concept of the division of labour was now well-established.

Late eighteenth century/nineteenth century
The Industrial Revolution altered the demographic structure of
Britain. Demand for low-cost fuel and a reliable water-source
brought industry to previously rural communities.

Twentieth century
The production line concept was introduced, each worker being
trained to perform a specific task. The production line depended
upon each worker knowing his/her role and contributing to one small
part of the production process continuously during a work shift.

Twenty-first century
The impact of the knowledge economy and of globalization is felt.
People start to accept that there is no such thing as a job for life.
Rising unemployment figures show the urgent need to keep
marketable skills updated.

Insight
> Many people still can't get their head around these changes –
> whether it's previous generations who have known stability
> of employment or young people who have not yet considered
> their future.

What is a job?

All these changes serve to reinforce a key point – that the 'job' is a
comparatively recent phenomenon. The first industrial revolution gave
an almost universal understanding of the concept of a job, as follows:

Insight
> The concept of a job:
> The social contract into which we enter with an employer
> to spend an agreed number of hours per week in his/her
> employment in exchange for a certain sum of money which
> allows us, within financial constraints, to spend it in the way
> we wish to pursue a particular lifestyle.

Because we or our parents may always have known a 'job', it is easy to forget that it is not something which has existed from time immemorial and which should always continue to exist as part of our social fabric. As we have seen above, until the Middle Ages, people certainly had work – but they would have looked at you askance if you had suggested that their work would always remain constant throughout their lives and that they would pick up a pension at the end of it. In certain ways, of course, these are concepts we are reverting to.

HOW JOBS WERE INVENTED

It cannot be over-emphasized that the 'job' is something which emerged with the Industrial Revolution. It was something which in a novel way appeared to offer security, compartmentalizing a large part of the day into a known group or sequence of tasks.

Recent experience of the job has been that, for those in a stable employment situation, the employer would ensure employment until retirement age. Yet for many people, there were no programmes of retirement planning. One day they would be in full-time work, the next day without work. Their final day in work would be marked by a party celebrating the loyalty and achievements of the individual, and with the presentation of a gift such as a gold watch to mark the transition from active work to retirement (literally 'withdrawing'). Surely, the symbolism of the gold watch was bizarre – the overtones of value, worth and treasure were also reinforcing the fact that now (perhaps for the first time in the individual's life) time did not matter! There were no fixed schedules or deadlines.

The decline and fall of the job

In the same way that the first Industrial Revolution of the eighteenth and nineteenth centuries had a major impact on people's lives, so too, we are undergoing another industrial revolution in the early years of the twenty-first century.

That initial premise of the job was based upon it remaining fixed within a certain and known world. Of course, dependent upon ability, hard work and opportunities, that job might evolve through promotion into a more prestigious and financially rewarding one – but not necessarily a more enjoyable one as we will see in Chapter 4.

What has happened to make job certainty disappear?

Daily, the numbers of people who realize that there is no such thing as a permanent, secure job swell. Whilst governments may talk of creating more opportunities for employment (and indeed have created some), there is no suggestion these days that full-time permanent employment for everyone will return. Indeed, ministers know that to do so would be unrealistic, insincere and unworkable as it would fly in the face of everything happening not just nationally but globally.

Insight

Both my parents and my parents-in-law (and others of their generation) would have been perplexed by these changes. Having survived the Depression of the 1930s they thought that work was secure and would have found current ideas of work disturbing and unsettling.

The reasons for such change are varied and complex and have evolved over different timescales. But in summary, there are six principal reasons why this has occurred.

1 THE DEVELOPMENT OF A GLOBAL ECONOMY

Consider how many of our consumer goods and indeed how much of our culture is now global. Wherever you go in the world, you will see young people wearing clothes or footwear with names like Adidas, Levi's or Nike. Whether it is in Europe, the Far East or the Americas, the goods will be the same. Adidas, a German company, produces its branded garments wherever they can obtain the right balance of cost and quality. The country of origin is immaterial. For example, in these post-Rover days, it is difficult to find any British-badged volume car actually built in Britain with the exception of the Vauxhall Astra (and Vauxhall is part of the US multi-national General Motors). British brand names and Fords are built abroad and some Japanese models (e.g. some Hondas, Toyotas and Nissans) are UK-built.

2 MANY JOBS ARE AT THE MERCY OF CHANGING CUSTOMER NEEDS

Until the 1970s, in any European port, a large number of dock-workers would be required to unload a ship's cargo. Today, most shiploads are containerized, requiring only a small number of highly skilled crane operators to move the container from ship to dockside storage to truck or rail-wagon from the comfort of an insulated cab high in the air. It is not that customers are saying 'We don't want to employ dockers' but rather that they want goods transported securely, safely and with the minimum of handling – with consequent savings in time, paperwork and cost.

3 TECHNOLOGY HAS ACTUALLY CHANGED THE NATURE OF MANY BUSINESSES AND INDUSTRIES

Substantial technological development allows companies to be more productive with fewer staff. Technology can help drive down costs and drive up consistency of quality. For example, motor manufacturers compare their efficiency on a global scale by quoting the number of labour hours it takes to produce a vehicle. The Nissan plant in Sunderland is currently the most efficient car plant in Europe.

Take a look in any newspaper or telephone directory for the number of financial services which can be bought 'direct'. From insurance to pensions and investments, many companies have established themselves to capitalize on the public's requirement for simplicity of service, longer opening hours and doing away with the customer's need to complete paperwork. In these 'call centres' employees, wearing a telephone headset and sitting in front of a computer screen, transact customer business. This is predicted to become a major form of employment, with many employees being part-time, working flexible or unsocial hours. In some cases, the growth in business crosses borders – a major US insurer uses a call-centre in the Republic of Ireland staffed by people several thousand miles from both headquarters and customers and a number of UK companies (e.g. National Rail enquiries, some BT customer services and Supanet, the internet provider) use call-centres in India. Likewise, in some cases, the work is not carried out by the company itself but is subcontracted to other companies, which is called ...

4 'OUTSOURCING' OF WORK

It is a rapidly expanding phenomenon that many major companies now retain a small core staff for regular operations and buy-in additional expertise and labour on a short-term or consultancy basis as and when it is needed. This way the company can reduce its payroll and on-costs, focusing its efforts on its core purpose. When it needs additional staff, it calls on a pool of people to whom it may pay relatively high consultancy rates to deliver specified services 'just in time'. When the contract finishes and the need no longer exists, the company no longer has to support these people through the lean times. For example, in the early 1990s, the Ford Motor Company in Britain needed to downsize to retain its competitiveness. This downsizing coincided with Ford's need to invest in new engineering as it had contracted to build new engines for international use, as well as enhancing its engineering to meet the demands of the recently acquired prestige marques, Jaguar and Aston Martin. Consequently, whilst the company had a programme of redundancy and early retirement for staff over 50, it also created a consultancy base through which it bought back staff on a consultancy basis. They were contracted over a short term for their engineering skills as and when needed but without the long-term commitment to an employee.

5 THE CONTINGENCY WORKER

Work, and hence employment, are dependent upon there being a demand for goods, products or services. As we saw earlier, if there is a change in consumer needs but no corresponding adaptation or flexibility from the employer, jobs are at risk. Everyone's work depends upon the organization achieving results. Of course, the first staff to go in difficult times will be the temporary, part-time staff but employers the world over are clapping their hands that even well-established, permanent staff can be lost when finances dictate. (Naturally, this can create major problems when economies or companies experience an upturn and don't have the expertise or experience on tap – but that's a separate issue.)

6 A CHANGING MINDSET

As organizations become aware of their own fluctuating needs and of how their own long-term strategic planning is limited because of external factors, so they have started to buy-in staffing on an 'as and when' basis. These are not unskilled, casual staff brought in by the holiday trade for the peak summer months. The 'new' workforce may:

▶ *be highly intelligent, gifted creative individuals*
▶ *be well-qualified and*
▶ *have a wide range of experiences and expertise which can be tailored to the specific needs of the organization buying in such consultancy – whether short term or long term.*

These are people who know, understand and value their own skills and expertise and can also sell these skills to the appropriate bidder. They put their own personal progression and employability at least on a par with the organization's objectives.

In short, these changes require a fundamentally different outlook on the world of work. From the static, secure world in the early part of the chapter, we have moved into a world where the essential qualities and skills needed to remain in employment are characterized by William Bridges in his book *Jobshift* (see 'Taking it Further', p. 198) as Employability, Vendor-mindedness and Resiliency.

What does Bridges mean by these terms? Let us summarize what he is saying:

- ▶ 'Employability' *is retaining your attractiveness to employers by developing and displaying those abilities and attitudes in demand.*
- ▶ 'Vendor-mindedness' *involves starting to think as an external consultant who has been hired to carry out a specific task.*
- ▶ 'Resiliency' *is fairly self-explanatory, requiring the individual to be able to find his/her own security from within, by knowing his/her strengths and weaknesses rather than being dependent passively upon some external agency (the traditional employer).*

Insight

So, to pick up the theme of this book, *employability* is a combination of the changing mindset and the contingency worker within the global economy.

Restructuring the workplace in the twenty-first century

Restructuring organizations was a major activity of the 1990s, although in recent years the focus has changed. Initially, the purpose was to 'downsize' at all costs – to shed excess capacity, labour, plant and sites in order to achieve a 'leaner, fitter structure'. More recently, the focus has been upon business process, performance improvement and to involve and integrate employees in this exercise. In particular, the principal reasons cited for restructuring now tend to be: meeting customer needs, strategic planning and teamworking.

Clear lines of accountability are also important and this has been seen in the public sector with changes to pay and conditions such as 'The Agenda for Change' in the National Health Service (NHS) and the restructuring of staff (according to identified teaching and learning responsibilities for teaching staff and the assimilation of grades for non-teaching staff) in state schools across England and

Wales. For many staff in both services, this is a new and sometimes alien work ethic.

Flexibility in employment is a key objective – organizations need flexible employees to meet the demands of today's customers for round-the-clock delivery of products and services. This is why some organizations have now introduced **annualized hours** or **job-shares** to give that mutual flexibility. It does not just affect the private sector – many part-time college lecturers will be on annualized hours, with their teaching 'front-loaded' so that they are not needed (or paid) during the summer examination period.

But flexible employees are also needed to be responsive to changing demands, to take on a wider range of roles and tasks, to switch from project to project at short notice and yet be able to hit the ground running. All this requires competence and confidence in the skills and qualities which may not have been in demand previously.

HANDLING THE ISSUES – THE GOVERNMENT RESPONSE

Such major changes as those outlined mean that governments must conduct a radical overhaul of the infrastructure of the tax, social security benefits and contributions systems in order to reflect the flexibility and uncertainty in the labour market. For example, in the UK the unfunded liability for public sector pensions is now about £800 billion – which must fall on taxpayers in the decades ahead.

Government figures show that more of us are living longer and that this trend will continue. Figure 1 shows the projected life expectancy beyond the age of 65, based on age-specific mortality rates at each age for each relevant future year.

UK population	Cohort life expectancy on reaching age 65 in the year shown (years)					
	2008	2015	2020	2030	2040	2050
Women	23.3	24.1	24.6	25.4	26.3	27.2
Men	20.8	21.7	22.2	23.1	24.0	25.0

Figure 1 Projected life expectancy at age 65 (Source: Pensions Policy Institute, 2006).

With such challenges in strategic, long-term planning for business, health-care, education and other areas of life, governments are asking questions such as:

▶ *How will people's pensions be paid?*
▶ *How can there be an equitable pension treatment for those in the private and in the public sectors?*
▶ *How can the tax system track the variety of activities in which people may be involved?*
▶ *How does the school education system shift from preparing pupils with high levels of static academic knowledge to a flexible working and learning environment in which teachers can no longer sincerely say 'Work hard, get your qualifications and you'll get a good job and a secure career'?*
▶ *How does the education system respond to individuals' needs which do not follow the neat pattern of academic years and terms?*

HANDLING THE ISSUES – THE PERSONAL RESPONSE

For those of us who have been made redundant, 'outplaced', had contracts terminated, reached the end of a fixed-term contract or otherwise been dispensed with, the feelings can initially be complex and difficult. You can feel rejected or marginalized – both personally and professionally; that your professional expertise and experience is not valued and that the organization's values have diverged widely from your own. You can feel that all the hard work over many years, the loyalty, devotion, goodwill, extra hours and effort, the placing of the job or organization above your own personal or family concerns have counted for nought.

You may ask: 'Has the way in which I handled this contract; achieved that target; dealt with that tricky situation; trained those people; implemented this change or become an integral part of the reason that people want to do business with this organization stood for nothing?'

In the words of a former colleague, 'Working for this organization involves give and take. You give, they take.'

Facing up to the issues

You can sense a range of emotions – not least at the varying degrees of competence with which change management and matters of outplacement have been handled by those who have no conception of the personal feelings of those involved. Indeed, you can question in a professional context the competence of those remaining. 'What valuable skills does X have which I do not possess?' Perhaps X does indeed have specialized skills or a level of competence from which we could all learn. Or perhaps X has been in post so long that it's going to cost too much to make him/her redundant when normal retirement age is just around the corner. Situations like this can be complex and difficult to analyse and cope with on a personal level, particularly when it is unlikely that you will have at your fingertips all the relevant facts upon which corporate decisions have been made.

Increasingly, there is alarm in the UK about the cost of pension provision in the public sector. In an era of people living longer and longer, the number of people active in employment (and who will be called on to pay for the state pension) is diminishing rapidly, putting an estimated additional burden of £30,000 on each household to pay for this provision. In 2010 there are 4.1 British workers per pensioner but there are forecast to be fewer than 3.5 by 2020 and just 2.8 by 2030. (Source: *Daily Telegraph*, 8 May 2010.)

Insight

As I write this in spring 2010 we are in the midst of a General Election. Many politicians argue that the public/private sector pensions apartheid needs to be addressed. In an age of increasing longevity, the nation can no longer afford them and change (for new entrants at least) must come. The simple question is – would you prefer to be poorer in retirement ... or dead?

What is clear from the above is that people will have to work longer in order to receive less in pension payments – so we may as well do work we enjoy!

And, of course, we must remember that for some people, the offer of early retirement, voluntary or compulsory redundancy will be eagerly grasped. They have had enough of that organization and are ready for a change, or for a break from or an end to work. They may take away with them a negative attitude to work and are sufficiently comfortably off not to bother with it again. Good luck to them. Such people are a dying breed, both in terms of attitude and financial well-being – and they are unlikely to be readers of this book.

But those for whom a new stage in life beckons and who want to approach work in a more pro-active way than previously, this book is going to help build upon those skills and experiences.

Self-check questions

If you have been in one of the situations described above, it is important to reflect upon and to discuss your personal response. You may already have done so – with former colleagues, in the pub or with friends and family. But many people do not discuss the issues of how they feel. Before we proceed, it is important to get such feelings in the open, otherwise they will be at the back of your mind when we are trying to move forward. You can simply jot some points down in the gaps or use the questions as a trigger for a discussion with someone whose opinion and listening skills you value.

If you have been made redundant or outplaced, how do you feel about:

▶ *The way in which it was done?*

▶ *How it affects your attitude to work?*

(Contd)

▶ *How it affects your attitude to life?*

▶ *How it affects your opinion of yourself?*

▶ *How you feel about future prospects of work?*

Case studies

Throughout this book, we will follow the progress of three
fictional characters – Jane, Francis and Ramish – as they develop
their employability skills. The first set of case studies will examine
the family influences on their understanding of jobs and work.
These powerful influences are what psychologists call 'scripting'.
Sometimes we have to 're-script' ourselves. This requires changing
the values and expectations which we have of ourselves and which
our cultural influences (family, friends or workplace) may have had
on us. We're going to follow how far our three characters change.

JANE STARTS OUT ON HER CAREER

Jane comes from a traditional middle-class British background. Her
father was a civil servant who remained with the Department of the
Environment all his working life, straight from grammar school.
He progressed through the different levels of the Civil Service to
a middle management position. His income was sufficient that his
wife did not have to work and she was encouraged to stay at home
to raise the family. The family atmosphere was a secure one, based
on the dependability of Jane's father staying in that secure and
relatively unchallenging environment. Yes, there were pressures

periodically, but nothing undermined the notion that her father was an indispensable servant of the people, working in a world somewhat aloof from the perceived 'unpleasantness' of industrial and business life.

Jane consequently grew up in an atmosphere that valued security, avoided risks and expected the state to provide in the future in return for loyalty at work. That embossed crown on her father's briefcase symbolized the dignity and permanence of his employment. Indeed, Jane's friends who were the children of the self-employed or of those in business were regarded as somehow being a little flash.

Jane begins to feel the pressure

Having completed a B.Ed. degree in a respected Higher Education college, Jane commenced her teaching career well-briefed on the National Curriculum, classroom control and motivating primary school children. But she was not prepared for the mountain of paperwork involved in assessment and reporting, which she saw grow over the years. Recognizing that, compared with many other jobs, teaching occupies only 36 weeks of the year, she is also aware that during term-time she puts in a 10-hour day on average.

FRANCIS FOLLOWS IN HIS FATHER'S FOOTSTEPS

As a child Francis lived in several parts of the country, following his father's employment as a sales representative with a major insurance company. Accustomed to the commercial aspect of life, Francis recognized that there could be peaks and troughs in the company's performance. Fortunately, they were shielded from the troughs and his father went from strength to strength, although his mother would usually have a part-time job just to be sure. There was an expectation that if you fitted in with the company ethos, it would look after you in the bad times and that future provision was a mixture of company and personal prudence. Francis remembers the long days his father would spend at the office, the sales conferences and the week-long training programmes. 'Work hard', 'abide by the company rules' and 'don't get caught out by using your initiative' were the golden rules his father had instilled in Francis.

Certainly, when Francis finished his compulsory education, he had little inclination to progress to further or higher education. 'I'm just delaying getting a job', thought Francis and he saw how, with his head screwed on the right way, and by taking his family's values into the workplace, he could also prosper with his chosen career in the Eastern Bank.

Francis feels adrift

It came as something of a shock to Francis when his bank was taken over recently by a larger institution. The rather cosy world in which he had immersed himself since leaving school disappeared overnight, as did several of his older colleagues for whom the prospect of major change was too much. Francis had not realized how steeped he was in company tradition until the clash of cultures with the new company was on him. How would he fit in? Could he adjust? How did other financial institutions operate? What was the new script?

RAMISH BREAKS WITH TRADITION

As the son of first-generation immigrants, Ramish was aware of both cultures. Leaving India had been a bold decision for his parents, but based on the promise of a better and more secure lifestyle in Britain and better financial rewards for those who tried hard. Ramish saw this in older relatives who had arrived in Britain a few years earlier – 'Work hard and you will achieve'. Yes, there might be some racial prejudice but there was always work available and Britain seemed to value the ethos of a determination to do well.

Those first few years were tough – a succession of dingy bed-sits whilst the family established itself. Ramish remembers his childhood, living above the corner-shop which had become the family's business. Working 18 hours a day, never taking holidays and the gradual decline of his mother's health were the penalties. But the close community respected the level of service, the chance to buy goods on the slate and the way in which all the family would contribute to the enterprise by delivering shopping, running errands and so on.

From these humble beginnings Ramish saw that there was hardship and suffering among his community and determined that when he grew up, he would help do something to relieve the hardship.

The attraction of working for the National Health Service (NHS) was obvious to Ramish. It offered a quality and breadth of provision he marvelled at and also the opportunity to contribute to society he had yearned for since his early years. Qualifying as an osteopath, he started his early career with great enthusiasm and ambition, which served him well for many years.

Ramish senses disillusionment setting in

However, as he progressed up the career ladder, he also became aware of the new 'managerial ethos' and how the focus was much more upon achieving managerial and business targets in an environment which had no control over the quality of its raw products, i.e. patients. Disillusionment and disenchantment were setting in fast.

THINGS TO REMEMBER

We have:

▶ *Outlined the reasons for the end of the permanent job.*

▶ *Thought about how this affects your current situation.*

▶ *Defined the concept of employability.*

▶ *Looked at case-study examples of the effect on people in positions possibly similar to you.*

▶ *Stressed the importance of sharing your thoughts and feelings on these issues.*

ACTION POINT

▶ *Identify someone with whom you can discuss these issues.*

2

Getting to know yourself – what you are

In this chapter you will learn:
- *about what you identify as key milestones in your life*
- *about the influences people have had on you*
- *what different roles you play in your life*
- *how to make a PEST of yourself*

Charting progress

How did you become what you are today? Whatever stage of life you have currently reached, there have obviously been powerful influences which have brought you to this stage. These might be educational, sociological or anthropological. They might include influences from family, your peer group, previous employers or other sources. It can be enlightening to reflect on these and to consider how they have influenced us to become *what* we have become.

Insight
In knowing what we are, we are in a stronger position to determine what we might become.

MARKING MILESTONES

For this next activity, picture in your mind two educational experiences you have had – one good and one bad. These experiences can be from any part of formal education at primary, secondary or other education or training. For example, it could be improving your numeracy skills, learning to drive or learning to crochet. It could be a formal learning situation or an informal one. It really doesn't matter as long as you can identify *one* situation in which you feel you learned a lot and *another* in which you feel you learned little.

For instance, taken from school, an example of the first experience might be: 'We had just started algebra and I found the concepts really difficult. The teacher sat down next to me, gave me some individual tuition, patiently explaining it for several minutes. Then everything clicked.'

Or for the second experience, 'One day the teacher left the classroom for a few minutes and, on returning, found that a lot of pupils were playing around. The whole class was put in detention even though I was getting on quietly with the work set.'

Remember that although these experiences are taken from school, your experiences can be from any aspect of your own education or training.

RECALLING EXPERIENCES

To help you visualize the experience, try to picture the teacher/tutor/trainer in your mind.

> **Recall experience 1**
>
>
>
> **Recall experience 2**

Having recalled both experiences, try now to assess *why* you have recalled them.

▶ *What is it about these two experiences which sticks in your mind?*
▶ *What do they tell you about the way you learn or respond to learning?*
▶ *What do they tell you about the way you are motivated or demotivated?*

Insight

People in some societies, perhaps, are more used to being told what they can't do rather than what they can do.

CONSIDERING YOUR ACHIEVEMENTS

Moving on from this, let's now consider some of the real achievements and milestones in your life to date. Frequently, when we think about achievements, we tend to think only in terms of educational achievements (the number of exam passes etc.). Without devaluing the importance of these, particularly if gained as a mature student in difficult circumstances, they represent only one aspect of our lives. Indeed, the psychologist B.F. Skinner said that 'Education is what remains when what has been learned has been forgotten.'

How many other things may we have done where we have felt that there has been no formal recognition of our achievements? Remember that the British educational system traditionally worked by setting up barriers (e.g. the eleven-plus examination) for most people to fail at in order that only a few could excel. Examples of achievements outside education might include: learning to swim as an adult, acting as a peacemaker between squabbling family members, redecorating the lounge – at last.

Insight

I am constantly surprised that many young people who have just left compulsory and post-compulsory education

(Contd)

have little sense of what they have really achieved. Yes, academic qualifications should rightly be celebrated. But other achievements are important also. Completing a Duke of Edinburgh Award or military training, for example, say so much about determination, tenacity, overcoming adversity, showing initiative and other attributes. Do we give these achievements sufficient recognition and status?

Identifying those who have influenced you

From time to time we reflect upon those who have in some way influenced us to make the decisions we have taken in order to become what we are. We know those who have influenced us directly or indirectly, the way in which they may have inspired us, energized us or encouraged us to take some decision or action. They might be family or close friends. Equally, we may not have known them personally – they might be religious or political figures, authors, management gurus or sports people.

The poet Thom Gunn used the title *My Sad Captains* (from Shakespeare's *Antony and Cleopatra*) to describe those whom he admired and who influenced him during their lifetime. In this poem, they appear almost like ghosts but shining out in the darkness with the brightness and presence of stars. They appear to have the strength of will and perception not to be caught up in the detritus of petty occurrences, but to stand as a beacon of light and influence for those needing guidance and support.

Consider who in *your* life has influenced you, acted as an enabler, opened your eyes or in some way had a lasting impact on the way in which you have evolved. Jot down who these people were and how they may have influenced you in some significant way. If you wish, you can add to the list, but keep it to those who have really had an influence on you.

Those who have influenced you:	How they have influenced you:
....	....
....	....
....	....
....	....
....	....
....	....
....	....
....	....
....	....
....	....

SELF-CHECK QUESTIONS

▶ *Would those who influenced you understand the situation you are in now?*
▶ *If so, how would your 'sad captains' be speaking with you now?*
▶ *What advice would they give you now that you are considering this change in your life?*

Identifying what you do

Whatever actions have led us to our current situation, much of our life may now be spent carrying out different tasks in particular roles. We each have different aspects to our total being which cumulatively make us the people we are. What might these different roles be? For example: colleague, line-manager, trade union official, parent, brother/sister etc. We sometimes use the expression: 'Wearing my ... hat, I think that ...'. Different roles call for different actions and attitudes and these can sometimes cause conflict. For example, we may sometimes have to discuss with a colleague his or her work performance and perhaps we have to criticize it – poor punctuality, missing an important meeting, ignoring a deadline etc. It can be hard to do this, yet at the same time it is both expected of us and will certainly cause more trouble if we do not tackle the situation in the early stages before it becomes a real problem.

Yet when that colleague is also a friend, it can be more difficult still. Which hat do we wear – that of friend, colleague or boss? Do we swap hats at stages during the discussion? If, when wearing a manager's hat, we have had to criticize someone, how do we ensure that when we next see him or her at a social gathering that he or she knows we are wearing a different hat? Of course, style of conversation, facial expressions, body language, postural mirroring and context can all give the necessary signals. Even so, making the switch between roles – changing the hats – can cause stress.

FILLING IN THE LABELS WITH THE ROLES YOU HOLD

Identify your own 'hats' or roles. Here are some examples:

mother	colleague
father	boss
son	manager
daughter	junior
brother	trade union representative
sister	team leader
relative	team member
husband	opposite number
wife	mentor
partner	role model
home maker	coach
cook	paymaster/mistress
taxi driver	appraiser
counsellor	appraisee
mender of broken hearts	student
teacher	contractor
customer/client	

Maintaining your employability

BEING A PEST

Predicting the future is an inexact science, to say the least. There can be many factors which bring about or influence changes, as we saw in Chapter 1. A helpful way of trying to assess and understand the likely trends and developments in your own employment sector is to carry out a **PEST analysis**. This may help you get a greater understanding of what is happening and where your organization thinks it is going. Useful sources of information can be company newsletters, news items in the media about your sector, websites and internal memos and notices about changes.

A PEST analysis considers in sequence the various factors which may have an impact upon your sector and your own organization:

- ▶ **P**olitical
- ▶ **E**conomic
- ▶ **S**ocial trends and
- ▶ **T**echnological.

Hence the title. Understanding these can give you a clearer sense of what is happening to the organization and, through that, a clearer understanding about your own situation in the workplace.

CREATING A PEST FOR FRANCIS

Let's look at this below and see how such an analysis might inform one of our characters, Francis, who works in the financial services sector.

Political changes
These changes include legislative changes, requirements to meet European Community standards and the likely impact upon society through a government's desire to bring about a particular change.

What does this mean for Francis? For the financial services sector, recent political factors would include:

- *the overhaul of the pensions system (simplifying rules and introducing SIPPS)*
- *the UK government bail out of many high-street banks, and*
- *abolishing the Child Trust Fund.*

Economic factors

These factors would include the consequences of implementing an economic policy both nationally and internationally. For the UK this would include interest rates, the value of the pound sterling and the UK stock market; the rise in mortgage costs, the difficulties for exporters, the drop in the price of imported goods and the value of stock-market linked investments. Consequences of the political decision not to be in the common European currency (the Euro) would also be important.

What does this mean for Francis? This might have an impact on issues such as:

- *the number of mortgages his bank can sell*
- *the competitiveness of its savings products*
- *the growing globalization of financial services through mergers (e.g. Banco Santander's acquisition of high-street names like Abbey, Alliance & Leicester and Bradford & Bingley), or*
- *the outsourcing to India of telephone banking services.*

Social trends

These may be directly out of political hands but they would reflect the changing mores and culture of the country. To ignore these would be fatal for any organization.

What does this mean for Francis? Notable trends include:

- *flexibility of pension schemes*
- *flexible 'Australian type' mortgage products which take account of the uncertainty of employment*
- *the desire by people to conduct their financial transactions 'direct' during evenings and weekends rather than during a hectic day or rushed lunchtime*
- *the loss of faith in financial institutions after the global collapse of so many banks and insurance companies.*

Technological

This is self-explanatory, as we saw in Chapter 1 (e.g. the use of call-centres and the containerization of goods in transit). Information technology (IT) skills are important for all workers now at whatever level and those remaining Luddites are doomed to extinction. Accessing the internet to settle a credit card bill or using a phone banking service clearly has implications for staffing levels.

Additionally, it means that staff training and development is now frequently online or web-based and can be accessed on-demand, so Francis has less need to travel to 'away days' or residential courses. Such training can be done 'on the job' and there is an increasing expectation that technology can provide much training. For example, some companies are placing all training on audio-only MP3 players – overlooking the limitations that exist in learning through a single medium (i.e. in this case only through hearing). Nevertheless, many organizations are using 'blended learning' – a mixture of learning styles and modes of attendance (including distance and online learning) – hence the expression 'clicks and mortar' learning.

For Francis, these changes mean:

- *getting to grips with IT*
- *ensuring that customer service is as quick, thorough and efficient as possible by using this technology*
- *ensuring that technology is not off-putting or worrying to customers who distrust computers*
- *adapting to the impact of IT on his own professional training needs and future working pattern.*

Here is how Francis's PEST looks.

- **P**
  Responsiveness to legislation.
  Responsiveness to partial public ownership.
  Preparation of and familiarity with new products
  (e.g. stakeholder or SIPP pensions).
- **E**
  Products matched to customer needs – has bank grown and diversified too quickly?
  New constituency of customers.
- **S**
  Changing demography.
  Different working hours?
- **T**
  IT skills.
  Online business.
  Customers' expectations of a rapid, accurate turnaround of documentation.
  Change in training expectations and ethos.

CREATING YOUR OWN PEST

Having seen how Francis might complete a PEST reflecting changes in his working environment, try devising one for yourself in your working environment. There is a blank template below for your use.

```
P ·························································
·
·
·
·
·
·
E ·
·
·
·
·
·
S ·
·
·
·
·
·
·
T ·
·
·
·
·
·
·
·························································
```

Being a rounded person

People often feel that all that employers are looking for is
someone who can carry out a specific role or function within
the organization – to wear a particular hat. But, as we have just
seen, none of us ever wears just one hat. Some people, particularly
the self-employed and those with a portfolio career, are changing
hats frequently. Even for those in traditional employment, some
jobs require frequent changes. Take a secondary school teacher,

for example. Every 35 minutes, he or she will change roles to take a different class each comprising individual pupils with individual needs; each time the bell sounds the lesson content will be different, needing to be pitched at different levels; every lesson the group dynamics and class management skills will be varied in order to present an accessible yet challenging learning environment. Perhaps the teacher teaches several subjects, changing from RE and Sociology at A level to lower school English. Each pupil will see the teacher differently and will recall experiences of help, advice, encouragement, praise or castigation. Some will have seen him or her on the sports field, in a drama production, or on a Duke of Edinburgh Award weekend etc. Is it any surprise that teachers can often feel so physically and emotionally drained, maintaining all these separate yet complementary interactions?

Yet, as we have seen with the example above, when a school appoints a teacher, it is not merely seeking a teacher of subject X. It is seeking a team member, someone who will volunteer for out of school activities, someone to bring expertise and understanding of children, ideas, equipment, finance or administration as well as subject knowledge. It is all too easy for employees in any field to forget that employers will take the overview of the total contribution to the organization an individual can bring.

Rating your confidence in your employability

Now it is time to turn to the way you respond to the prospect of retaining and developing employability in *what* you are in your own organization. How positive or confident do you feel about your employability with your current employer? Read through the table below and score yourself accordingly.

How confident are you about your current employment?

I feel of value and know that my skills and knowledge are in demand. I can see progression opportunities within the organization. Should there be organizational changes I know clearly what I want and am confident of having the right skills to offer. I am confident that I can create and gain fulfilling work within the organization.

Positive

Currently my work and role are valued. I have the necessary skills and aptitudes to perform other organizational roles. My future within this organization is uncertain and I have no clear sense of either who to talk with or what I should do if my post disappears.

Unsure

There is uncertainty about my current post. I worry about the future because I don't think that I have the right contacts, skills or aptitudes to achieve a post I want here. Nevertheless, I recognize that I have plenty to offer and I'm keen to learn.

Anxious

My skills are solely job-specific. If this post goes, I don't know what else I could do. I feel very pessimistic about getting another job with this organization and don't know what they could give me. I have never been encouraged to think about what else I could offer. Is it too late now?

Negative

Now think about how confident you feel about applying for posts with other organizations.

How confident are you about applying for posts with other organizations?

I am alert to the employment market in my sphere. I am confident that I could gain fulfilling work with another organization. I am pro-active and constantly seeking ways to develop my employability and to creating opportunities for myself.

Positive

I have a reasonable understanding of the employment market – enough to know where my strengths and weaknesses are. I don't like the idea of change but am sufficiently realistic to grasp the opportunities offered to me.

Unsure

I have always developed job-specific skills but can see now that I need to develop a wider range of skills and qualities. I am concerned that I won't be able to do enough quickly enough to catch up.

Anxious

When I look around the employment scene I feel that I have little to offer someone else. My skills and abilities don't seem to be in demand. I am very worried about not having employability skills.

Negative

INTERPRETING YOUR RESPONSE

If your personal confidence rating has been low in either case, this book will help you enhance your confidence as your skills develop. If you scored yourself in the top half of the scale, the book will assist you to maintain your employability.

··

Insight

Notice that in each case the more positive responses go hand in hand with a pro-active frame of mind – seeking and creating opportunities and taking the initiative. The more negative responses are accompanied by a more passive and reactive role – waiting for others to do something.

··

Case studies

JANE CONSIDERS HER PLACE IN THE TEAM

Jane has now been teaching for some years. She has never felt inclined to seek a promoted post and has consequently not taken on additional duties voluntarily. Her experience is limited to a single school and to a single job. Of course, being a classroom teacher *does* demand adaptability, flexibility, resourcefulness, initiative and good interpersonal skills. But Jane is also realizing that there are other skills she lacks – she is not a very good team-worker (preferring to be left to get on with things on her own), and she tends to rely on the Head or Deputy telling her to do things on a school-wide basis.

FRANCIS REFLECTS UPON HIS PEST

Francis has now worked for two major financial organizations. His qualifications and hard work implementing company policy to the letter served him well under his previous employer. He was aware of all the financial regulations and good practice and dutifully attended job-specific training courses when required. His new employer has a different approach: it prizes customer focus, independent thinking (provided it is within the regulations), lateral thinking and initiative. We know that Francis finds this hard. Yet friends in other financial institutions tell him that it's the same anywhere. Francis does not feel confident about rediscovering the old ways with any other employer, let alone landing promotion with his employer. Still, only 19 years, 7 months, 23 days to go.

However, Francis has now completed his PEST (see p. 30) which has shown him what the likely developments are going to be. He now has to face whether to work with these and keep ahead of the game or to be swamped by the changes.

RAMISH RECOGNIZES HIS WORTH

Ramish has always made full use of all staff development opportunities offered to him, whether in work time or in his own time. He has an impressive range of skills and experiences as a result and has also picked up several professional qualifications. His work within his field has been recognized at a professional level by being asked to speak at several influential and prestigious conferences and his professional views are sought by colleagues. All this has involved extra work, not freebies. Certainly, it impressed his employers who felt that he was suitable for several forthcoming vacancies. They considered themselves lucky that they appointed him to his current position, as a neighbouring health authority has just come up with a similar post, but on a higher grade. It's probably not worth the extra travelling time and expense for Ramish to consider this one. Lucky that he's just settled into his post now – he would be a great asset to lose.

THINGS TO REMEMBER

▶ *The milestones in your own development.*

▶ *The people who have influenced you and their impact.*

▶ *The roles you have in aspects of your life.*

▶ *Your PEST analysis.*

▶ *How you rate your own future employability.*

ACTION POINTS

From what your PEST tells you about the future of your employment sector:

▶ *What appears positive about this?*

▶ *What opportunities might this present for you?*

▶ *What appears negative about this?*

▶ *What concerns might you have?*

▶ *What action do you think you should take to enhance your employability?*

3

Getting to know yourself – who you are

In this chapter you will learn:
- *about the significant events which have shaped your life*
- *how to distinguish your needs from your desires*
- *how being aware of these factors helps you create change*

Starting to feel comfortable with being you

So far we have seen some of the major changes affecting the idea of employment and have considered the impact which this has upon people in work. In the last chapter we considered the various factors which have brought you to the position you now occupy as an employee or potential employee (in other words, *what* you are now).

In this chapter we are going to look at some of the factors which have made you the *person* you are today. If we can understand ourselves, we stand a much better chance of finding a working environment which shares those values.

How often when we meet someone do we ask them *what* they do? Even where the discussion is not related to our work or workplace, we often don't converse in general. We gradually move the conversation towards 'jobs', not only to find some common ground but also to see where we may be in the employment 'pecking order'. In Western society we can be obsessed with workplace-based notions of comparative status, and perhaps no country has been as obsessed with this concept as Britain! No wonder other nations have found Britain so class-riddled. As such, our conversations can become stilted by focusing too much on what people are rather than *who* they are as individuals.

> **Insight**
>
> It is helpful to understand this 'who you are' idea before you can consider how to gain the most benefit from the opportunities which lie ahead of you.

In order to consider who you are, you need to reflect on your past life.

Life-mapping

The following activity is a very practical one designed to help you understand how you have reacted to some of the most significant events in your life to date, and how those experiences may affect your response to change now or in the future.

Below is a sample **life-map**, in this case belonging to Ramish (the osteopath in our case studies). Ramish was asked to identify the most significant events in his life (both positive and negative) and to list them.

Here is Ramish's list:

1 *Enjoyed primary school where I set my sights high.*
2 *Started secondary school – intimidating atmosphere and made to feel insignificant. Determined to prove teachers wrong.*
3 *Got good O level results – chose science A levels, intending to read medicine.*

4 *Grades not good enough to get into medical school. Selected osteopathy at a college.*

5 *Enjoyed college and socializing.*

6 *Fell deeply in love with Prakesh, who then rejected me.*

7 *Got first job and bounced back from disappointment in love by proving competence in work.*

8 *Death of father. Plunged into grief but eventually emerged with new vigour.*

9 *Met Mia. Best thing that's ever happened.*

10 *Promoted into management – frustrated and feeling trapped.*

Ramish then plotted these events on a graph, indicating their relative positive or negative rating. His graph is shown in Figure 2.

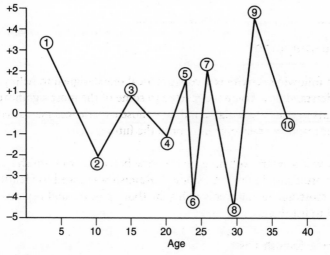

Figure 2 Ramish's life-map.

Below is a blank life-map. Complete the table in chronological order with your own significant events – you may need to reflect carefully on some of these as some events will come to mind more readily than others.

MAKING YOUR OWN LIFE-MAP

1

2

3

4

5

6

7

8

9

10

Now complete the numbered events on the grid in Figure 3, adjusting the age scale to your own circumstances.

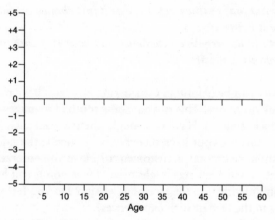

Figure 3 Life graph for self-completion.

WHAT DOES THE CHART SIGNIFY?

If we look at Ramish's list of events, we can see a mixture of positive and negative experiences, the degree of positive or negative rating being apparent from its position in the grid. What is noticeable is that, for Ramish, each negative experience is followed by a positive experience. For example, his sense of inferiority at school is accompanied by a determination to do well; his disappointment with his A level results is followed by a successful college course; his rejection in love is countered by the success he found in his work; and the loss of his father enables him to develop new priorities in life. His current situation (frustration in his work and what he gains from it despite his promotion) may be overcome by the closeness of the love and support of Mia who may spur him on to other things.

Your chart may not look like this. Negative experiences may not be mirrored by positive subsequent experiences. However, look at your negatives where they occur. Ask yourself:

- ▶ *Did the negative episodes have a learning experience for you?*
- ▶ *If so, what was the positive to emerge from this?*
- ▶ *How did that positive occur – was it just chance or did you make it happen?*
- ▶ *What did the negative experience and your response to it tell you about yourself?*

This activity can be helpful in considering how you have responded to previous situations. This is what some football managers call 'bounce-back-ability'). Have you sought shelter from such painful changes by turning your back on everything outside the safe routine you have become accustomed to? Have you embraced the opportunities which change might offer? Have you learnt how you react as an individual in the face of adversity? Do you feel stronger or weaker in the face of such experiences?

Preparing for the future

The next step is to prepare for future situations. The following activity is designed to help you project forwards to enable you to consider how you might want to spend the rest of your life. This is important for assessing your own employability skills because it will help you come to terms with what you want from life, including what you want from work. This activity requires you to think carefully about your dreams, your needs and how you might achieve them. The activity will take you about twenty minutes but you need quiet and to be able to concentrate. You will also need a pen or pencil. (If you are on a train or plane with enough time before your journey finishes, you'll be able to do this.) If you cannot do so at this stage, put the book aside and plan a time when you can complete the task in one go. Don't skip the activity and read ahead – you'll lose out on a crucial step.

Identifying your needs and desires

We often think we know what we really want. Few people would turn down a lottery or pools win. Few of us do not dream of holidaying in some exotic location. But for many people these desires are unachievable. The exotic holiday is part of an imaginary lifestyle. The pools win is a catalyst to a lifestyle rather than a desire in itself. At a more mundane level we might desire a new iPod, the latest wide-screen TV or a ride-on motor lawnmower. All of them are 'merely' materialistic *desires* – we can live without them and most of us do so.

Insight

Indeed, rather than having what we want, it's a question of wanting what we have.

What we are considering here is what actually drives our innermost *needs*. For many people, these needs can be independent of financial situation (as long as we are not in poverty). For others, the financial imperative is still there (why do 'fat cats' insist on high bonuses even when they may have phenomenally high salaries anyway?). For others, there are more spiritual or literary/artistic drives. Some people need to feel a sense of power or control. Some people are gregarious and always need other humans around them whilst others prefer a more solitary existence. Some people need precise, ordered systems by which to live their lives, whilst others prefer an element of disorder. We are all different and no one way is more 'desirable' than another. (We will look at these human needs in more detail again in Chapter 4.)

Listing your needs and desires

To plan the next stages of your life, you need to understand what might be the differences between your desires and your needs.

We have seen how far the three people in our case studies have been scripted and the courage it is taking them to come to terms with re-scripting. Here is an opportunity for you to develop your own script.

To help you do this, imagine what you will be doing in the future. Often when we do this, we close our eyes. For obvious reasons you cannot do so now! Nevertheless, try to imagine the next stages of your life and to picture a *typical* day over three timescales:

What will you be doing in 12 months' time?
▶ *What will your life be like?*
▶ *What will your work be?*
▶ *Who will be the important people in your life?*

You may find it useful just to jot some points down in the space here.

When you have completed your mental picture, ask yourself: How different is 12 months from today? Is it simply projecting your existing life a year ahead? Maybe you have pictured your children as a year older and at a different phase of their life? Maybe relationships with loved ones have changed. Some of these we might take for granted given the passage of time. But how are *you* different? Have you noted any major or minor shift in you?

What will you be doing in three years' time?
▶ *What will be a good day at work?*
▶ *What do you associate with satisfying work?*
▶ *What would be a good day outside of work?*
▶ *What factors will be absent?*

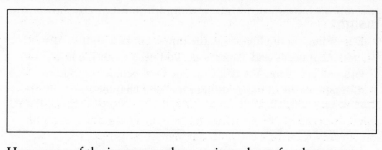

How many of the images you have written down for three years hence are linked with those for 12 months' time? Are there similarities or have you moved on in your thoughts? Perhaps 12 months is too short a timescale to achieve what you really want but there are some glimmers of that achievement over a three-year period. How many of these things have come about by chance and how many because you have been pro-active in making them happen? And if you have been pro-active, when did that process start? What are some of the small, perhaps seemingly insignificant things you have done to cause this to happen? Has it been, for example: planning your activities, prioritizing demands or saying 'no' to people?

What will you be doing in ten years' time?
▶ *Where will you be living?*
▶ *What might a good day consist of?*
▶ *What experiences would be pleasurable to you?*

Has there been any shift in your images over this period of time? It would be extremely unlikely if there had not. Some of these may be dependent upon your age now. How do you get from now to then?

Depending on the life-stage, the time-span and your own individual needs and aspirations, you need to decide how you will get there. We will examine how people respond to different forms of motivation in the next chapter.

How will you be remembered?

It may seem a rather strange and even unpleasant notion but, if you were to die tomorrow, how might you be remembered? In his famous poem *Afterwards*, the English poet Thomas Hardy imagines seeing the aftermath of his own death, with his idea of what people will say about him. Although Hardy was much more than a nature poet, focusing in his novels on the struggle of humans against a sometimes tyrannical and harsh concept of Fate, the lines quoted below give an indication of some of the qualities and characteristics which Hardy felt he possessed:

Afterwards

When the Present has latched its postern behind my tremulous stay,
And the May month flaps its glad green like wings,
Delicate-filmed as new-spun silk, will the neighbours say,
'He was a man who used to notice such things'?

If, when hearing that I have been stilled at last, they stand at the door,
Watching the full-starred heavens that winter sees,
Will this thought rise on those who will meet my face no more,
'He was one who had an eye for such mysteries'?

Clearly, Hardy sees himself as observant, perceptive and attuned to the natural world with time for animals and nature.

My epitaph

Now, here is your opportunity to confront yourself with how you think people will remember you tomorrow.

As you consider your own achievements, don't fall into the trap of mere 'conventional' achievements such as just listing your qualifications or projecting your perceived status in terms of job title. They may say *what* you were but not *who* you were. As the old joke goes, very few people die wishing that they had spent more time at the office.

Think also of the things which you had wanted to achieve and believe that you have achieved. Again, this will give you an idea of your values, or what you hold dear in life, of the things which you are prepared to give time and effort to in your life.

You can, if you wish, complete the template below to write about yourself. This is how you see yourself at the moment.

The death of (name) .... (aged).............. has just been announced. S/he is remembered principally for endeavouring to ....

....

....

S/he had always wanted to ....

S/he will be remembered for her/his contributions in the sphere of

....

(Contd)

and will be remembered by .... and .... because of her/his ....

If you were to write about yourself in 12 months', three years' and ten years' time, how might the memories of you be different? How much would you have achieved of the, as yet, unfulfilled ambitions and needs?

You can, if you wish, develop this into an open epitaph written on the outline headstone in Figure 4.

Examples can be seen in the case studies below for our three characters who are beginning to reflect upon their past experiences and to plan their futures.

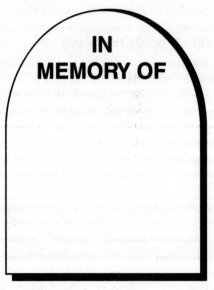

Figure 4 Analyse your needs and desires by writing your epitaph.

Case studies

JANE DIPS HER TOE IN THE WATER

Jane is doing much the same now as at the end of Chapter 2 but she has become more adventurous in her hobbies and outlook. She has decided to present some of her craftwork at the forthcoming school fete and is hopeful that this will attract orders from parents as well as flag up to the school in a public and visible way her latent talents in other areas. Jane realizes that in her own experience, her solid school exam results meant that she was expected both by school and parents to pursue a higher education course and that she chose teaching for negative reasons – she had no strong desire to do anything else. The range of achievable possibilities was not presented to her and with her 'civil service' family background, it seemed safe to go into teaching.

FRANCIS FEELS OUT OF HIS DEPTH

Francis' relatively modest school career meant that he had little prospect at the time of progressing to higher education. The bank seemed a safe and relatively prestigious career. Steady progression up the career ladder was achieved by equally steady, if unstimulating work and by adhering closely to the bank's procedures. Francis became viewed as a 'company man', well-versed in policies and procedures, always checking with the handbook if a problem arose. As a matter of principle, he referred upwards any matters outside the scope of the handbook, thus ensuring that he could not be accused of using his initiative. On reflection, this had made him inflexible and reactive when the company was taken over and the new culture prized the ability in junior managers to use a quality which had never been previously encouraged – initiative. That meant taking risks and having opinions, and after 15 years, this wasn't something Francis took to easily. Francis realizes that he has reached a plateau in his career. What can stimulate him now?

RAMISH HAS DOUBTS ABOUT THE FUTURE

The son of a first-generation immigrant family from the Indian sub-continent, Ramish is rightly proud of his educational and career achievements, despite a few hiccups along the way. Compared with some of his distant relatives, he has done well and enjoys a comfortable lifestyle. He's got where he has through hard work, determination and undoubted ability. His latest promotion into management was applauded by colleagues and family alike but he is not certain that it's taking him in the direction he wants to go. Ramish has had to make hard choices or accept what appeared on the face of it to be a second-best solution previously (going to college rather than to university and being rejected by Prakesh). But he has always seen the positive aspects to come from such situations. He also feels that his career progression at times may have been at the expense of family relationships.

THINGS TO REMEMBER

In this chapter we have considered:

▶ *The significant events which have shaped your life-map.*

▶ *How positively you respond to negative experiences (your 'bounce-back-ability').*

▶ *Distinguishing your needs from your desires.*

▶ *How you would like to be remembered (values and principles).*

▶ *How your awareness of these issues can shape your future ideas of what you need from work.*

ACTION POINTS

▶ Given the changes you can see beginning to come over Jane, Francis and Ramish, what changes can you feel beginning to come over you?

▶ How far do you think that you have been in control of your own life or career so far?

▶ What can you do to take more control of your own life and career from this point? Make a list of the points.

The next chapter looks in more detail at how individuals respond differently to styles of working and will analyse which style motivates you.

4

Motivation at work

In this chapter you will learn:
- *about some of the main theories of workplace motivation*
- *how to identify what motivates you in work*
- *how employers use a range of strategies to motivate staff*

What motivates me?

In the previous chapter you have had an opportunity to consider some of the factors which have made you the person you have become. You have also considered some of the changes which might come about in the future to help you achieve the sort of lifestyle you seek.

Linked with this is an understanding of the sort of things in the workplace which motivate you – in other words, what makes you tick. Different people are motivated by different things, precisely because we are all different. For example, some people thrive on change and constant new challenges. For others, these constant changes would be very unsettling and, once they have mastered certain tasks performed in a set way, they don't like to see any alteration to this.

Employers can also adopt a variety of approaches to staff motivation, depending on how deeply they understand the needs of the workforce or whether they consider that each employee shares the same motivating forces they do.

In order to understand what motivates people, it can be very
illuminating to see what some of the principal organizational
psychologists have discovered through their research over the
years. We're going to look at some of these findings now.

Elton Mayo – acknowledging the human element

Elton Mayo and his team of psychologists conducted some famous
experiments in the 1920s and 1930s on 20,000 Western Electric
employees at their Hawthorne plant in Chicago. These became
known widely as the Hawthorne experiments. A series of tests
involving changes in working conditions (hours of work, length
and frequency of breaks and, ironically, lighting conditions etc.)
were carried out.

The research team noticed that when the adverse changes were
explained to staff, when staff felt involved in the process and
felt valued as employees, then any such changes did not reduce
production levels. Indeed, production rose to an all-time high
and absenteeism reduced by over 80%. Where employees had
their conditions changed with no consultation or explanation and
where no one attempted to make the employees feel valued, then
production and efficiency both dropped. Mayo's team concluded
that production levels were influenced by factors other than the
physical conditions of work.

What Mayo was *not* saying was that, as long as you are nice to
your employees, you can get away with anything. However, he did
highlight the importance of the human element – of clarifying with

employees the reasons for decisions, of involving them, of taking time to get to know them and explain. In short, by valuing the workforce you are more likely to get more from them – as well as a sense of loyalty, of commitment, of a sense of cohesiveness and self-esteem. Additionally, there will be lower staff turnover and a consequent reduction in staff recruitment and training costs.

Such a 'human relations' approach stressed the importance of work groups, relationships, leadership and personnel management in enhancing motivation and understanding organizational behaviour.

SELF-CHECK QUESTIONS

In your experience of work:

▶ *How often have major changes affecting your work been explained to you?*
▶ *How have you felt if such changes have not been explained?*
▶ *What strategies do you adopt for informing or explaining changes to your colleagues, suppliers, customers etc.?*

Abraham Maslow – satisfying inbuilt needs

Maslow (1908–1970) argued that all people have what he called 'a hierarchy of needs'. In other words, each group of needs is at a different level. He identified these needs as:

▶ *physiological (bodily)*
▶ *safety*
▶ *social belonging*
▶ *esteem*
▶ *self-actualization, by which he meant realizing one's own full potential.*

These needs can be represented as in the pyramid in Figure 5.

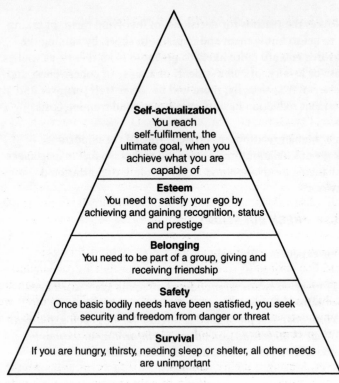

Figure 5 Maslow's hierarchy of needs pyramid.

Self-actualization
You reach self-fulfilment, the ultimate goal, when you achieve what you are capable of

Esteem
You need to satisfy your ego by achieving and gaining recognition, status and prestige

Belonging
You need to be part of a group, giving and receiving friendship

Safety
Once basic bodily needs have been satisfied, you seek security and freedom from danger or threat

Survival
If you are hungry, thirsty, needing sleep or shelter, all other needs are unimportant

Maslow's reasoning was that once an individual's physiological needs have been satisfied (warmth, food etc.), the individual then becomes more concerned with a safe environment. Once this need has been achieved, the individual progresses to concern with a sense of belonging to a community (such as a partner, a family, a social or religious grouping). Beyond this level of need, Maslow argued that individuals need a sense of esteem – of self-worth. They like to feel valued and to have a role or series of roles, whether these are played out in a relationship, in the community or in the workplace. Right at the peak of the pyramid, Maslow contended, was the need for self-actualization – and it is only here that an individual's true potential can be released.

NEEDS DIFFER ACCORDING TO CIRCUMSTANCES

In essence, what Maslow states is that people's needs differ according to their circumstances at any time. For a starving African, the notion of self-actualization is of no consequence when one's whole being is consumed by desperately craving food. Like all living beings, the most important need is to have sufficient food and water for survival. Once this is achieved, the next stage is to seek refuge (perhaps from the rebel dictator's forces who are carrying out 'ethnic cleansing'). Having achieved this level of basic survival, the individual can now focus on the remaining human needs – of social belonging and so on. Thankfully, for most people we know, the bottom two categories in the pyramid are easily satisfied. If we are hungry, we eat and we are merely reminded of the need to do so periodically during the day by slight pangs of hunger. For most of us, satisfying this need is not a problem and we can focus on other needs in our lives, perhaps even experiencing real fulfilment. But for the homeless person or substance abuser we pass on the street, a great proportion of the day will inevitably be spent in meeting urgent physiological and safety needs.

However, Maslow's theory reminds us that there are some people who can transcend these needs, despite the circumstances. Gandhi, for example, existed on a poverty diet whilst making his protests about British rule in India, and yet he was able not only to dream of but also to achieve self-actualization by gaining independence for his nation.

Nevertheless, one of the most important tenets of Maslow's view is that, in general, Western society is very good at meeting the lower three needs in the hierarchy – physiological, safety and social belonging. What Western society is not so good at, he maintains, is giving people esteem and allowing people to self-actualize. Whilst Maslow did not envisage that his theory should necessarily apply to the workplace, it certainly remains one of the most well-known theories used by some managers.

Insight

'Never go back.' If you have moved on at work, re-visiting a former job or employer can be deflating. As part of one job, I needed to visit a previous employer and, whilst there, I called in to see former colleagues – at the same desks, complaining about the same issues as 15 years previously. None had moved on. Calling in was a mistake and unsettling – I didn't need reminding how much more fulfilling my working life had become.

Clayton Alderfer – levels of need

Alderfer reduced Maslow's hierarchy to three levels, known as 'ERG'. Note that these are presented in reverse sequence to Maslow's ascending pyramid.

▶ Existence needs. *These include physiological and material desires and equate approximately to Maslow's first two levels.*
▶ Relatedness needs. *These social needs cover the third Maslow level and part of the esteem needs concerned with personal relationships from level four.*
▶ Growth needs. *These incorporate the remaining needs from level four and the self-actualization needs.*

Alderfer suggests that lower level needs do not have to be satisfied before higher level needs have a stronger influence. But it does suggest, for the employer, that if an employee's growth needs are limited because the job itself does not foster opportunities for personal development, then the employer should provide greater opportunities for the other groups of needs to be satisfied.

SELF-CHECK QUESTIONS

▶ *When was the last time you were thanked for completing a task well, or on time or under-budget?*
▶ *How much scope do you have with your current employer to develop both professionally and personally?*

- *How far do you agree with Maslow's classification of needs?*
- *Can you identify any skills or attributes within yourself which you are keen to bring to fruition in the workplace?*
- *Can you identify any skills or attributes within yourself which you are keen to bring to fruition in your social life?*

Douglas McGregor – alternative ways of managing people

Influenced by Maslow, Professor McGregor (1906–1964) became President of Antioch College in Ohio. He was particularly interested in the way in which managers treated their workforce and how different management approaches determined different responses. He argued that there are essentially two ways of managing and motivating people, and he termed these Theory X and Theory Y.

Theory X is the authoritarian style. This is based on the assumption by managers that people:

- *are lazy*
- *dislike work*
- *need a mixture of carrot and stick to perform*
- *are immature*
- *need direction*
- *are incapable of taking responsibility for their own actions.*

This style of management prevailed, for example, in the British car industry during the 1970s.

Theory Y assumes the opposite. It is based on the assumption by managers that:

- *the average human being likes work and gains satisfaction from it*
- *in the right conditions, people will voluntarily set themselves targets*

- *encouragement and reward are more effective than threat and punishment*
- *people learn not only to accept responsibility for their work but will actively seek it.*

Japanese-owned or -influenced car industries reflect this approach with employee involvement through 'quality circles'.

Of course, we must recognize that effective management involves sophisticated and complex tasks requiring a range of approaches and styles to be deployed. Even the most enlightened and ardent advocate of Theory Y recognizes that, in order to ensure quality and consistency, you have to be firm and demanding on occasions.

Insight

For the manager or leader, this is where skills and emotional intelligence come into play – knowing how and when to apply such an approach requires a sound understanding of people. You might like to look at www.businessballs.com for an interesting diagrammatic illustration of these two theories.

SELF-CHECK QUESTIONS

- *Considering your current (or past) employment, in what ways have you experienced a Theory X manager?*
- *Considering your current (or past) employment, in what ways have you experienced a Theory Y manager?*
- *In which employment culture do you work better, X or Y?*

Frederick Herzberg – identifying the sources of motivation and demotivation

During the Second World War, Herzberg was a US Army sergeant who witnessed the Dachau death camp. This experience triggered his interest in human motivation and he became a psychologist. Working with his research colleagues, Herzberg interviewed over 200 engineers and accountants in the United States in the late 1950s. They discovered that there was a great similarity in the aspects of their work that these employees found motivating or demotivating. These are shown in the 'content theory' of motivation chart.

Sources of job satisfaction (Motivation factors)	Sources of job dissatisfaction (Demotivation factors)
1 Achievement	1 Company policy/administration
2 Recognition	2 Supervision
3 Work itself	3 Salary
4 Responsibility	4 Interpersonal relations
5 Advancement	5 Working conditions

For many people, the sources of job satisfaction (**motivation factors**) are powerful. Even small elements of these factors can make a significant difference to the way they feel about and respond to work. The sources of job dissatisfaction (**demotivation factors**) are often areas over which the individual has traditionally had little control, the climate and culture of the organization dictating the working practices.

Herzberg argued that simply giving a pay rise would not solve the underlying problems. The pay rise would rapidly become the norm and the real problems would remain. This was an issue which both British motor manufacturers and the automotive unions repeatedly failed to recognize during the 1970s, as is shown in the case study below. Herzberg also promoted the ideas of job enlargement, job rotation and of the 'cafeteria' system of benefits. These again were ignored. However, in time, his 1968 publication *One More Time, How Do You Motivate Employees?* sold 1.2 million reprints by 1982 and was the most requested article ever from the Harvard Business Review. Real change in attitudes towards work occurs only when workers become involved in taking decisions. A brief case study illustrates this.

Recognizing values

In the mid-1980s a large building society took over a smaller, regional one. The new culture (*company policy/administration*) had a rigid structure with decision-making being very much 'top-down'. Many former employees of the small building society found difficulty in adjusting to this inflexibility and rigidity. Those who had been allowed a certain autonomy and discretion in their work now felt that they were closely supervised and could no longer be trusted (*supervision*). Whilst the new society paid more, many employees preferred a slightly lower salary with greater autonomy (*salary*). The larger, more formal ethos of the organization made interpersonal relations more difficult at all levels (*interpersonal relations*).

Consequently, the former employees of the small society felt that the working environment (*working conditions*) was worse than their previous employment – particularly with regard to the IT system which was poor and a source of major frustration.

As a footnote, the organization concerned obviously needed to rationalize its branch network and workforce, calculating that they needed to lose 200 staff. However, they were inundated with 1200 requests for redundancy, indicating widespread discontent and little opportunity for job satisfaction!

Insight

I was working with a quango about to be absorbed into a government department. I knew that I would find a petty politicking, 'Yes, Minister' atmosphere enervating and soul-destroying. Preferring 'a bias for action', I focused instead on developing work outside this environment and have never regretted it.

> ▶ *How does your personal list of motivation factors compare*
> *with those identified by Herzberg?*
> ▶ *How does your personal list of demotivation factors compare*
> *with those identified by Herzberg?*

How motivating employees can rescue an industry

The British car industry in the 1970s was in serious trouble. The
quality of design, production and technology was poor, as was quality
control. Working practices in the industry were old-fashioned and
strikes were common. The British Leyland company (the forerunner
of Rover) had nearly 200 disputes in one year alone. Unions tried to
outdo each other in achieving the highest wage settlements.

However, the real problem was not money itself. The wages were
really regarded as being compensation to the assembly-line workers
for the extremely tedious, repetitive and soul-destroying nature of
work on the production line. Employees had no say in suggesting
improvements or in the overall efficiency of the company.
Furthermore, they had no voice to make their concerns known,
other than through the unions – which shared management's
view of pay levels being the root of all concerns. Jobs were rigidly
demarcated. If, for example, an assembly worker noticed that a
conveyor belt needed oiling, he would have to ask a skilled fitter
to do it. There was no way that job demarcation rules allowed him
to do it himself even if he was able and willing to do so, an oil-can
was in reach, or that it would add a little variety and responsibility
to his job.

Only when British companies began to adopt Japanese working
practices (e.g. the collaboration between Rover and Honda
on developing new models), did satisfaction levels increase
and productivity improve. Such working practices include:
active maintenance, quality circles, quality control mechanisms
throughout the manufacturing process and establishing a

culture of trust, involvement and customer satisfaction through communicating with the workforce.

Today, things are very different. Some companies, such as Ford, have Employee Development Assistance Programmes (**EDAP**). These organizations believe that workers who are fulfilled mentally and creatively will be more productive and will contribute to the company as fully-rounded individuals. Consequently, each Ford employee is entitled to a £200 annual allowance to spend on any activity, provided that it is *not* work-related training (this being catered for separately). Likewise, in the public sector, organizations such as Nottinghamshire Healthcare NHS Trust also support staff learning activities to a maximum of £150 annually per person. In such programmes, courses as diverse as conversational languages, basket-weaving and learning to parachute have been undertaken. Of course, there have been a variety of factors other than motivating the workforce which have saved the motor industry. But this illustration proves beyond any doubt that Mayo, Maslow, McGregor and Herzberg were right in their studies and that people do respond to different management styles.

Insight

I recall several colleagues saying of their line manager that he felt that any real power and opportunity he had in order to make things happen had been taken away by the managerial climate. Instead, he acted as though the only power he actually had was to make others' lives difficult. Little did he realize the impact this had on his team.

Case studies

JANE REALIZES THE VALUE OF CONSULTATION

Jane started her career just after the implementation of the National Curriculum. At the time, such a framework for teaching seemed to her and other new teachers to be very desirable. You were told *what* to teach and could then concentrate on *how* you were going to teach it. She couldn't understand why so many of her colleagues were alienated or depressed by it, nor could she believe what she was told about the high number of headteachers seeking early retirement. As she has gone through her career, and has been part of the 'slimming down' of what became an unwieldy curriculum, she has begun to see how important it is for professionals to be consulted and involved in decisions about the curriculum. Even if Jane now sees her future outside of teaching, she has learnt the crucial nature of professionalism and that, to achieve change, consultation with people who feel passionately about what they are trying to achieve in their work is vital.

FRANCIS IDENTIFIES HIS PREFERRED WORK ETHOS

As Francis looks back over his career with the bank, he sees how the management culture of the former owners did not encourage him to develop or express his opinions, to become involved in decision-making or to suggest ideas or improvements. He regarded himself as a good employee, who meekly did as he was told, going by the book and without challenging anything or anyone. No wonder he didn't take to the new owners' style: suggestion boxes, customer clinics, focus groups – all 'trendy talking shops'. But beneath the gizmos, he could see that the new regime actually took the feelings and aspirations of both employees and customers seriously and that for new, young employees, the bank was a good employer. For those 'rather long in the tooth' with 20 years' experience like himself, it was too painful to change, to admit weaknesses and to develop a sense of ownership of his own aspirations and career.

RAMISH REJECTS THE EMPLOYER'S ETHOS

Ramish has always enjoyed the practical and professional aspects of his work and knows that he is good at them. It's the managerial ethos he cannot come to grips with. He entered the National Health Service believing it *was* a service with the needs of the patients paramount. But in recent years, he has felt that the system has lost sight of this and is playing at being a business with its 'commissioners' and 'providers', its 'client-led ethos' and its new managers who have been brought in from the private sector. He's all for efficiency and effectiveness and would be the first to aim for high professional standards. But he doesn't think that the NHS is a caring organization any more – it seems to be more about satisfying the needs of chief executives and departmental heads than anything to do with patient care. The workload for everyone has rocketed, and staff at all levels now have little time to talk with patients, to reassure them or allay their fears.

THINGS TO REMEMBER

We have considered:

▶ *Some of the principal workplace motivation theories.*

▶ *Your own workplace motivation factors.*

▶ *Your own workplace de-motivation factors.*

▶ *The way in which many employers have identified and built on the importance of employee motivation.*

▶ *The balance of activity you need from work to motivate you.*

ACTION POINTS

Everybody is motivated by different factors. After reading this chapter:

▶ *What factors can you identify as very important to your attitude to work?*

▶ *As a summary, what personal ambitions and aspirations do you have for your work?*

(Contd)

▶ *How far do you feel these can be achieved:*
  – *in your current employment*

  – *if you change employer*

  – *if you become self-employed*

▶ *What are the barriers to you realizing these aspirations?*

▶ *What are you going to do about these barriers?*

5

Understanding what you have to offer

In this chapter you will learn:

- *what 'transferable skills' mean and why they are important*
- *how to identify and develop your own transferable skills*
- *how to create your own SWOT analysis*
- *how to describe your own personality*

Understanding what employers seek

The early chapters of this book have reinforced the idea that the old covenant between employer and employee has broken for good and that *your future lies in your employability*. It is not up to employers to provide that which they can no longer do – the onus is very clearly on the employee, on *you*, to make yourself employable in this fast-changing and increasingly complex world. Many employers have changed this employment covenant with their employees and worked hard with them to make them understand. Others have changed the covenant – but just have not told the employees. Those employees who are unable to make this change will be the casualties not only financially but also in what they can get out of life in general.

By this stage, you should also have a clearer understanding of:

- ▶ *what makes you what you are (Chapter 2)*
- ▶ *what makes you who you are (Chapter 3)*
- ▶ *what motivates or de-motivates you (Chapter 4).*

We are now going to move forward to consider, firstly, the *skills* and, secondly, the *qualities* you have to offer.

Developing your transferable skills

Let's look in more detail at the sorts of skills which employers consistently say they seek.

Transferable skills are those skills which we can take with us from job to job, from task to task or from context to context. They can serve us well in life and are skills which we develop throughout our lives – there is never any stage when we become absolutely perfect communicators, for example. We refine and enhance those skills constantly through practice and by facing new situations and challenges.

In today's working environment, it is essential to be able to use a wide variety of skills and to have the confidence to do so. We need to be able to offer such a range of skills to potential employers or clients, as well as to our existing ones in order to ensure that we are able to undertake work of the highest quality and which is both challenging and fulfilling to us personally.

Employers are becoming much more specific and demanding in terms of the skills they seek. It is no longer good enough to approach an employer, saying 'I've got three A levels' or 'Here's my degree certificate in Biochemistry'. Whatever the level of employment and the nature of the work, employers need people who can:

- ▶ *work as part of a team*
- ▶ *communicate effectively in a variety of ways*
- ▶ *be confident problem-solvers*
- ▶ *take on a variety of complex tasks.*

THE INCREASING NEED FOR TRANSFERABLE 'KEY' SKILLS

The concept of transferable skills has become increasingly valued by employers *as well as* the qualifications, training and experience you can offer. Such a concept is still relatively new in many educational sectors – for example in both schools and universities – but it is something well-established in further education courses and more vocationally related higher education courses. For example, medical and nursing students will spend some of their course learning about 'bedside manner', breaking bad news or dealing with grief-stricken relatives; engineering students will focus on the 'professional skills' needed to become competent, communicative engineers and trainee lawyers will study how best to present a case eloquently to make maximum impact from a set of given facts.

However, many young people in schools and colleges now follow courses in Key Skills. According to the examination regulatory bodies in England, Wales and Northern Ireland, these key skills (called core skills in Scotland) are:

▶ *communication (more focused than English)*
▶ *application of number (practical application rather than theoretical mathematics)*
▶ *IT.*

Together with the 'wider key skills' of:

▶ *working with others*
▶ *problem-solving*
▶ *improving own learning and performance.*

It is recognized that not only are these skills necessary to survive and thrive in the workplace and to make the UK a competitive economy, but actually they underpin all other learning. Indeed, in some circles they are now being called 'essential skills'. Strange then that they should have been introduced only in 2000!

Employers are very positive about these skills, as they provide the sort of skill-set and mindset for a flexible and adaptable workforce. Many learners also have responded well to the challenges, particularly where they have developed them through project work. Universities, too, value the skills, given that students these days have to work far more independently than previously, need to access a variety of information in traditional and electronic format with confidence and are often required to make presentations. In some disciplines (e.g. medicine), students' ability to communicate effectively, to work as part of a team and to have skills in problem-solving is an important part of their skill-set to actually gain a place at university.

But, of course, not everyone has had the opportunity to gain such skills formally and, particularly for those who have been in the workplace longer, they may see new recruits with these skills as a bit of a threat. So what can you do to recognize and develop your own transferable skills?

Identifying your transferable skills

We do not always know what we are good at. Our families, teachers or employers have not always given us feedback on our strengths, perhaps assuming that we already knew these. Likewise, unless someone actually identifies and names a skill, we don't necessarily realize that's what it is, that's what it's called or that's what we can do!

A comprehensive checklist of transferable skills follows. Don't be horrified by the extent of them – anyone who can claim to have all of these skills developed to a high standard deserves a halo. Nevertheless, it can be extremely useful not only to understand what these highly-sought skills might be but also to consider how many of these we have and how we have developed them. Increasingly, employers may seek in written applications and at interview a self-awareness of such skills and qualities. Likewise, if you are thinking of going into self-employment, it is essential to have a clear sense of your skills and limitations. You will need an acute awareness of this in order to market your services or products, as well as marketing yourself. We'll look at this aspect in more detail in Chapter 7.

Comprehensive checklist of transferable skills

	Basic level [✓]	High level [✓]	Experiences which have developed these skills [✓]
Problem-solving ▸ *define and identify the core of a problem* ▸ *investigate what resources are available* ▸ *enquire and research into the available resources* ▸ *analyse data/information* ▸ *show independent judgement of data/information* ▸ *relate data/information to its wider context* ▸ *data appreciation: draw conclusions from complex arrays of data* ▸ *organize and synthesize complex and disparate data*			

(Contd)

	Basic level (✓)	High level (✓)	Experiences which have developed these skills (✓)
▶ apply knowledge and theories			
▶ show flexibility and versatility in approach			
▶ use observation/perception skills			
▶ develop imaginative/creative solutions			
▶ use an approach which is sensitive to needs and consequences			
▶ show resourcefulness			
▶ use deductive reasoning			
▶ use inductive reasoning.			
Team work			
▶ listen to others			
▶ be aware of own performance			
▶ observe others' performance and use perceptions			
▶ lead and motivate others			
▶ show assertiveness (set own agenda)			
▶ co-operate with others			
▶ negotiate and persuade			
▶ constructively criticize			
▶ produce new ideas or proposals			
▶ clarify, test or probe others' ideas or proposals			
▶ elaborate on own/others' ideas or proposals			
▶ summarize – bring ideas together			
▶ give encouragement to others			
▶ compromise, mediate, reconcile individuals and/or ideas.			

	Basic level [✓]	High level [✓]	Experiences which have developed these skills [✓]
Managing/organizing			
▶ *identify what tasks need to be done and the time scales involved*			
▶ *evaluate each task*			
▶ *formulate objectives, bearing in mind those evaluations*			
▶ *plan work to achieve objectives/ targets*			
▶ *carry out work required*			
▶ *evaluate and review progress and reformulate objectives*			
▶ *cope and deal with change*			
▶ *withstand and deal with pressures*			
▶ *ensure appropriate resources are available*			
▶ *organize resources available*			
▶ *show initiative*			
▶ *manage time effectively*			
▶ *demonstrate sustained effort*			
▶ *make quick, appropriate decisions*			
▶ *show personal motivation*			
▶ *execute agreed plans.*			
Communication (oral and written)			
▶ *explain clearly*			
▶ *deal effectively with conflicting points of view*			
▶ *develop a logical argument*			
▶ *present data clearly and effectively*			
▶ *take account of audience/reader in oral presentation/writing*			

(Contd)

	Basic level (✓)	High level (✓)	Experiences which have developed these skills (✓)
▶ show evidence of having assimilated facts			
▶ give appropriate examples			
▶ show enthusiasm and interest			
▶ show critical reasoning			
▶ use appropriate presentation techniques			
▶ compare and contrast effectively			
▶ listen and query where necessary			
▶ discuss ideas, taking alternatives into account			
▶ defend a point of view			
▶ assess own performance.			

As you read through the list, score yourself on how well-developed these skills are. Note down also the tasks or experiences which have given you these skills. These may be from your working life or from other activities. For example, being secretary of a local charity may have made you good at 'investigating what resources are available'; being a mother may make you show 'flexibility and versatility in approach'; or being a trade union representative may have made you able to 'listen to others'. We will return to your responses to this activity in the next chapter. But for now, let's move from thinking about skills to the personal qualities you have as an individual.

Insight

Many of us are used to carrying out SWOT or PEST analyses on our businesses. Indeed, they are a vital tool in staying ahead of the game. People do not always carry out individual

analyses on themselves, as suggested here. Try them – you
will be surprised how effective they are.

Becoming a SWOT

To consider the qualities you have to offer, you are going to have
to become a SWOT – but not in the old school sense. You are
going to carry out an activity which every business does about
itself in order to identify where it is now and where it is going.
By now you should have realized that you are a business – what
is sometimes called 'me plc' – the most precious and valuable
business you will ever be involved in.

However, here, your **SWOT analysis** is a breakdown of the
strengths, weaknesses, opportunities and threats of your particular
situation as a worker. It is what *you* have to offer. It is about you
personally, whereas the PEST analysis you did in Chapter 2 was
about your employment sector.

The strengths and weaknesses are *internal* – your inner qualities;
whilst the opportunities and threats are the *external* factors in
which you operate – your working environment. A blank SWOT
chart is shown in Figure 6.

Some people like to call it a SWOD analysis (strengths, weaknesses
and opportunities for development), but let's stick with the usual
term to reinforce the idea of you as your own business.

The idea is to honestly and openly appraise your own strengths and
weaknesses (SW) and to consider the situation you find yourself
in (OT). Positive aspects are on the left-hand side of the chart,
negative aspects are on the right.

For example, Jane from our case studies has drawn up the SWOT
chart about herself shown in Figure 7.

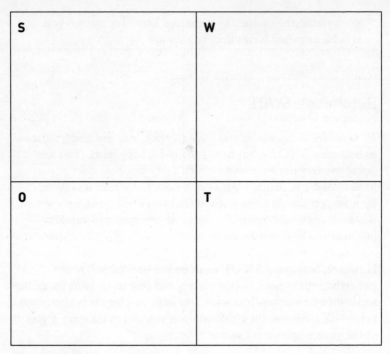

S	W
O	**T**

Figure 6 Blank SWOT chart.

ANALYSING JANE'S SITUATION

Analysing her situation in this way has allowed Jane to see clearly her strengths on which she can capitalize. Her level of education, receptiveness to new ideas, flexibility and adaptability mean that she is likely to be able to adapt to a new working environment. Her interpersonal skills would prove beneficial dealing with customers and suppliers. In particular, she is motivated by having control over her working environment which is likely to be the case in self-employment.

But Jane also recognizes her weaknesses – she hates computers and has had as little to do with them as possible (relying on her young pupils for advice!). She realizes that being within the same

S	W
Well-educated	Poor IT skills
Good interpersonal skills	Limited range of experiences
Flexible and adaptable	No experience of managing
Highly motivated in areas over	adults or finance
which I have control	Little motivation in areas over
	which I have no control

O	T
Skills outside workplace	More experienced competitors
Long holidays to develop	Can only exhibit during school
alternative work	holidays
opportunities	No alternative finance
Can operate from home	available
Could become supply teacher	
whilst establishing business	

Figure 7 Jane's sample SWOT chart.

job in the same school with essentially the same staff has limited her range of experiences and challenges. She has little sense of business although she takes great delight in working out how much profit her craft 'business' generates. What's more, Jane realizes that where she has not been fully involved in developments, initiatives or implementing changes in education she has found it hard to motivate herself.

Jane's perceptiveness in reaching these conclusions is not all her own doing. She has talked with and sought the opinions of her best friend Lindsey, who came to stay for a weekend. Jane trusts Lindsey's judgement and, having started her SWOT, Jane talked it through with Lindsey. Until this discussion Jane had not realized just how good she was in dealing with people until Lindsey reminded her of several situations at college which Jane had managed to resolve. Fellow students had looked up to her for this, which Jane had not known. Likewise, although Jane felt she was good at managing and motivating a large class of primary school pupils, Lindsey had to remind her that she had never 'managed' in the traditional sense – she had never had responsibility for finances, equipment, scheduling or other areas vital to the running of any business.

As for the opportunities and threats, Jane had also discussed her SWOT with her teacher colleague Ceri who understood the school culture in which they worked rather more fully than Lindsey who was a social worker. Ceri focused on the opportunities for Jane to develop her hobby more professionally during the holidays and also pointed out a teacher who had taken early retirement from a neighbouring school and who was doing well, albeit in a slightly different craft field. This was unknown to Jane, but was both an encouragement as well as a competitive threat.

REFLECTING ON JANE'S SWOT

With her list of positives (strengths and opportunities) and negatives (weaknesses and threats), the first task for Jane to consider is:

▶ *Is this an accurate reflection of her position?*
▶ *Is she sufficiently motivated by the positives listed to move forward?*
▶ *Is she sufficiently determined to address the negatives?*
▶ *If so, how can she turn the negatives into positives?*

Devising your own SWOT

Having seen how the process of devising a SWOT analysis works, now is the opportunity for you to devise your own. Think about the issues we have discussed in the previous chapters and your own response to these. Think about how Jane (who is perhaps a very different personality in a very different position) has gone about creating her SWOT. To help you:

▶ *Be prepared to take some time to devise your SWOT and to revise it in the light of reflection and discussion. The whole process might take you some days – even weeks.*
▶ *Identify someone/several people with whom you can discuss your SWOT. Choose people close to you whose opinion you value and who will give you an honest appraisal. This is not the time for false praise.*
▶ *Don't underestimate the power and value of this critical support.*
▶ *Think about as many aspects of your life as possible (the hats you wore in Chapter 2) to arrive at a rounded view of yourself.*
▶ *Assess whether you have the will-power to deal with the negatives as well as taking credit for the positives.*
▶ *Identify how you can turn your negatives into positives.*

Figure 8 is a blank SWOT chart for you to complete.

Describing yourself

In carrying out the SWOT analysis you have had to think about the sort of person you are. You have had to describe yourself. That is something which many people find difficult to do because they are not used to being self-critical.

Take the opportunity now to describe yourself *in three words only*, as:

▶ *an employee*
▶ *a colleague*
▶ *a partner*
▶ *a family member*
▶ *a human being.*

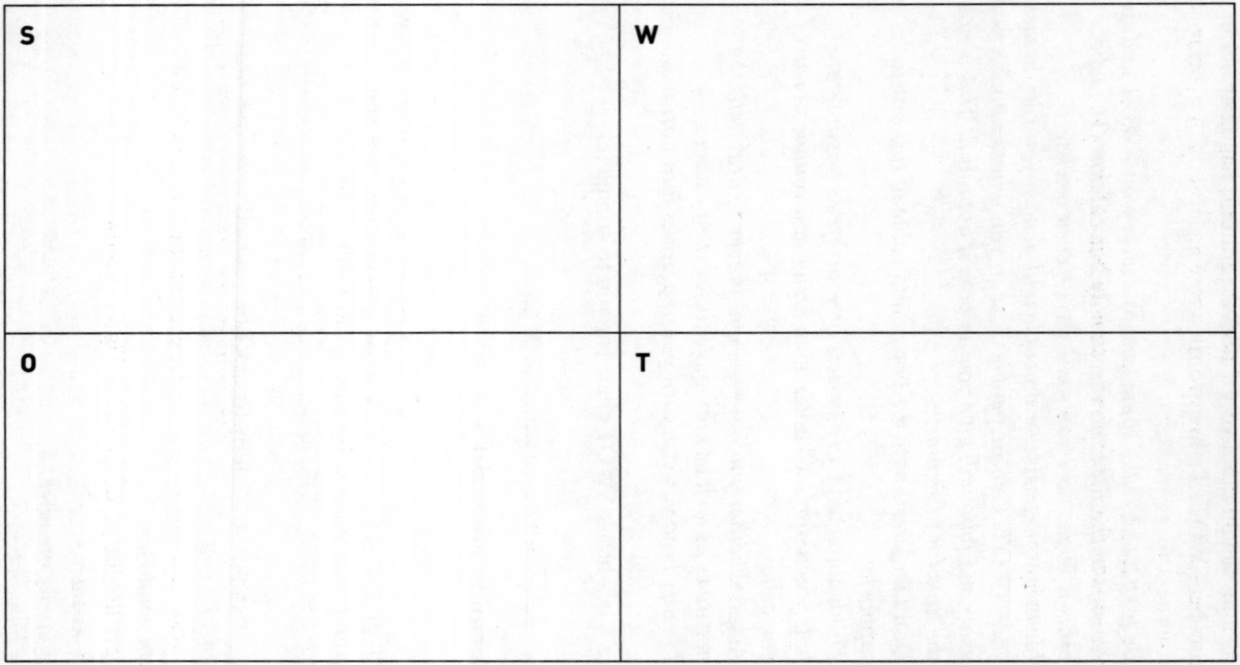

Figure 8 Complete your own SWOT chart.

S | W

O | T

Take as long as you need for the activity but don't agonize over choices – a gut reaction may be more accurate. Fill in your responses next to each category.

My self-description (three words only per category)

▶ *an employee*

▶ *a colleague*

▶ *a partner*

▶ *a family member*

▶ *a human being*

When you are ready to move on, read the information below.

Compare the list of adjectives in Figure 9 with what you have written about yourself.

- *Is there anything which you would add to your lists?*
- *Is there anything you would amend?*
- *Where there are 'different sides of the same coin' (e.g. a 'perfectionist' and 'pedantic'), which is the more accurate for you?*

> **Insight**
> As with the SWOT chart, you may find it useful to talk through your list with somebody you trust.

creative	adventurous	numerate
sensitive	thorough	cautious
organized	eccentric	able to plan long-term
prudent	aggressive	a bully
dynamic	extrovert	can see potential in people
assertive	gregarious	fair
patient	methodical	a good negotiator
flighty	compassionate	able to take an overview
persuasive	unpredictable	good interpersonal skills
generous	polite	self-aware
punctual	profligate	persistent
competitive	nit-picking	pedantic
quick-thinking	charismatic	financially astute
ambitious	loyal	prepared to take a gamble
timid	ruthless	unbiased
inconsistent	leader	sexist
single-minded	enthusiastic	able to plan short-term
cynical	reliable	egotistical
determined	flexible	authoritative
perfectionist	trustworthy	good time-manager
dependable	overbearing	able to delegate

Figure 9 Adjectives for self-description exercise.

Having examined all the possible words here (and any others you would add yourself), reduce this list to three words in total. These are the three words which, in any situation, you feel summarize your character most accurately. These are the words you can live with if they were to appear on a badge you wore. Transcribe these words on to your 'badge' (Figure 10) and keep these in your mind as we go through the activities in the rest of this book.

```
1

2

3
```

Figure 10 Your self-description badge.

Insight

Employees receive regular reviews or appraisals, which can be satisfying and rewarding experiences. As a freelance, you miss out on this, your skills and needs reflected only through self-perception and the fact that your business survives. When other people comment publicly on your abilities, it's rewarding and revealing, as their perspective can be far more positive and wide-ranging than expected.

Case studies

Each of our characters has now carried out a SWOT analysis like the one Jane did on p. 81. In order to move forward with their lives, they have to decide what, if anything, they will do about their weaknesses.

JANE BECOMES PRO-ACTIVE

Jane has decided to:

1 *Become more pro-active in her use of IT. Rather than relying on pupils to guide her, she has enrolled (at no personal expense) on an in-service computer training course.*

2 *Enrol at her local FE college for a part-time evening basic business management course designed specifically for those thinking of becoming self-employed.*

3 *Set herself the target of renting a stall at a craft fair in a neighbouring town during the next half-term holiday to sell her wares. Jane has two months of weekends and some evenings to create sufficient stock – a reasonable deadline which won't interfere with her school commitments.*

FRANCIS BITES THE BULLET

Francis found the SWOT analysis difficult to complete because he has not been used to thinking in a self-critical and evaluative way. Nevertheless Francis has:

1 *Had the courage to enroll on a weekend assertiveness training course at the local adult education centre. He has received full encouragement from his wife to do this.*

2 *Volunteered to be departmental representative on a working party. He hopes this will develop his communication and interpersonal skills as well as showing that he has a lot to contribute.*

RAMISH DEVISES A PLAN

Over the last few months Ramish and his partner Mia have spoken about the future on many occasions. However, they found the structure and discipline of the SWOT analysis helpful and enlightening. Although Ramish has thought and read extensively about a possible career change, he has now:

1 *Decided to attend a weekend conference on complementary medicine within the National Health Service.*

2 *Using his professional expertise and thirst for knowledge, approached a health service journal about writing an article on 'The clinical effectiveness of complementary approaches to osteoarthritis'. Whichever way his career takes him,*

Ramish feels that acceptance of this article in a prestigious journal can only do him good.

3 *Volunteered his services to his local GP surgery as a member of the Patients' Panel.*

In each case, our characters have identified ways in which they can move forward both personally and professionally. Notice also how they have made full use of the opportunities afforded to them by their existing employers or current employment sector. They are also starting to 'network' by making links with individuals or groups who may provide contacts in their personal or professional development. They are showing the additional skills and qualities which they have to offer their current employer, which is no bad thing if they should decide to stay where they are.

THINGS TO REMEMBER

We have considered:

▶ *Why developing your transferable skills is crucial.*

▶ *How to identify your current range of transferable skills.*

▶ *Devising your own SWOT analysis.*

▶ *Describing your own personality.*

▶ *Using feedback from others to clarify and confirm your skill-set.*

ACTION POINTS

▶ *Keep your own SWOT analysis up to date.*

▶ *Seek opportunities to enhance your transferable and other skills.*

▶ *Learn to read the developments and needs in your own organization as well as identifying how your skills and experience can transfer to other organizations.*

6

Developing your skills

In this chapter you will learn:
- *about the importance of communication skills*
- *about the importance of team-work and other skills*
- *how you can enhance your own skills-set*

Offering more than qualifications and experience

The world in which we live involves us carrying out a range of different roles simultaneously, as we saw in *The hats you wear* activity in Chapter 2 (p. 26). People may be involved, to varying degrees, in a variety of different tasks in which they have a specific role. The role may be different in each case, depending on the number of people involved – ranging from solo work to being part of a large team. However, maintaining this range of activities – this portfolio of employment – requires a clear understanding of one's own role as well as that of others, as well as the ethos of the organization/s one is working with.

In such a world, the way in which people interact with each other also changes. The traditional working environment has usually been as reflected in the *hierarchical organization chart* in Figure 11.

Your relative status is indicated by how far up the chart you are. Whilst the vertical channels of communication and responsibility are clear, the chart is static and inflexible. There are apparently no

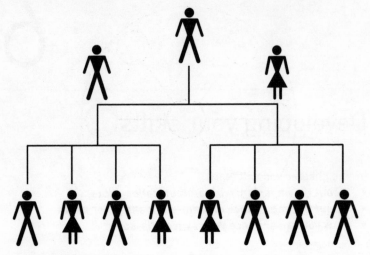

Figure 11 Hierarchical organization chart.

systems of horizontal communication with immediate colleagues or those in different disciplines (e.g. between marketing and production).

An alternative and increasingly common structure is that for *clusters of teams* within an organization, as shown in Figure 12. Here the individual teams have clear means of communication with fellow team-members and also down the spokes to a central coordinating body which ensures effective 'inter-cell' communication.

For the *freelance* consultant at the hub of the wheel in Figure 13, the structure will be different again.

The consultant makes contact down the spokes of the wheel with all his or her clients around the rim. Of course, to the client, the consultant is not at the hub of their wheel, but as outlined in Chapter 1, such consultants are brought in to perform specific tasks 'just in time' and are crucial at that stage. Inevitably, there is always some distance maintained between the hub and the rim, otherwise the structure collapses. Such a way of working is

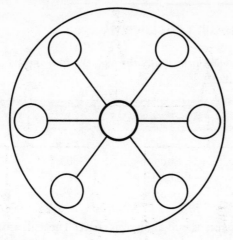

Figure 12 Inter-team organization.

increasingly common and some experts predict that by the year 2020, 20% of working-age people will be self-employed.

What is evident from any of these illustrations is just how important effective and clear communication skills and team-working skills are in today's working environment.

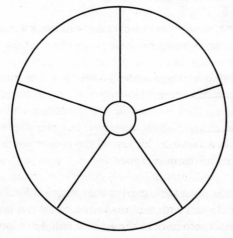

Figure 13 Consultant-based organization.

Communicating effectively

We communicate principally through the four means listed in the following table:

	Learned	Used	Taught
Listening	First	45%	Least
Speaking	Second	30%	Next least
Reading	Third	16%	Next most
Writing	Fourth	9%	Most

What strikes you as odd about this chart? The skill areas we teach are those forms of communication we use least (on average in Western society)! Of course, there will be exceptions – for example, people whose work depends upon frequent and sustained written communication. It is also true to say that the written communication of, say, a job application form or letter of application are perhaps some of the most important communications we make. But in ordinary social interactions, the degree to which we use a particular means of communication is in inverse proportion to its apparent importance of being taught!

As you can see, we are very rarely *taught* to listen yet we spend more of our time listening to other people than we do in any other form of communication. Perhaps because we can *hear* in the womb it is assumed that we know how to *listen*. Is it any surprise that we can often get things wrong? How often have you heard people say of others, 'He's a poor listener' or 'She never hears what I say'? Of course, we never say it about ourselves! In general, perhaps we do not listen as well as we could. List all the people you know who have been fired for listening too well!

To illustrate the point, let's carry out an activity. You'll need someone to help you with this, obviously. So, if it is not convenient at the moment, **come back to the activity and don't look at the following boxed section.**

Activity instructions

Ask someone to read out the following information to you. Listen carefully and make a note of anything you need to. You will be asked a question at the end.

You are the captain of a cross-channel ferry. On the first voyage of the day from Dover to Calais you have on board: 29 cars, 14 trucks, 2 coaches, 10 foot passengers and a total of 132 passengers.

On the first return voyage you have on board: 37 cars, 18 trucks, 4 coaches, 36 foot passengers and a total of 274 passengers.

Q: How old is the captain?

The answer you should come up with is obvious. But how often do we miss the first piece of information given to us – yes, you should have got it by now!

Networking

In essence, networking is simply a structured extension of developing your communication skills. We have already seen our three case studies starting to network with the decisions they took at the end of the last chapter.

What does networking mean? It means establishing who the likely opinion-formers and influential people in your preferred work sector are; it means getting to know individuals and starting to form relationships with them. Of course, no one likes individuals who force their way into a conversation, full of their own importance and of what they have to offer the world. Such an approach is likely to be counter-productive. But you have to be confident and assertive, as Francis has discovered. If you are not confident of what you have to offer, why should anyone else have faith in you, your specialist skills or knowledge, your product or your service?

Here are some suggestions for ways to network:

▶ *Identify the professional or trade groupings you need to work with and how they operate (conferences, trade fairs etc.)*
▶ *Pick up the phone to likely contacts and make your name known.*
▶ *Be persistent but not aggressive.*
▶ *Generate interest – once you have one contact, word of mouth can make the effect snowball.*
▶ *Start small and work up – if you have a product to sell at, say, a local farmers' market, the big supermarkets are likely to be more interested than if you have no customer base.*
▶ *Take calculated risks – if you attend just one convention, you will find out who the movers and shakers are, whether you have a niche expertise, product or service and whether you are cut out for such an endeavour, whether it be a business or a promoted post.*
▶ *Develop your emotional intelligence (see Chapter 7, p. 122) to maximize your impact and responsiveness to others.*

Many of the above suggestions will apply to making contacts in your preferred employment sector also.

How good are you at team-working?

At work you will often work with groups of others. Sometimes you might work with a team. What is the difference between a group and a team? Try to write a definition of a team in the following box.

> A team is

We all know what a team is in a sporting sense – a band of people with the same aims and goals, with complementary strengths and skills. The same is true of the workplace. Just as you don't expect in a sports team that all team members can excel in one particular aspect (e.g. all rugby players to be fast, light players on the wing, able to outrun their opponents rather than having a more supporting role, literally adding weight to the team), so different skills are necessary in the workplace.

Indeed, it is now accepted that in virtually all jobs, being an effective team-player is essential. Today's working world is too complex for the traditional workplace divisions and demarcations to operate. Many agencies operate multidisciplinary teams (e.g. in social work or health-care) so that holistic care and support is offered to a client/patient. Team-working skills are particularly important in small- and medium-size enterprises (SMEs) where employees can wear so many different hats during the working day. Even freelancers have to have effective team skills because, at times, they may be working collaboratively with other freelancers. Many broadcasters are freelance and, if you have ever been in a television or radio studio, you will know how a broadcast depends upon high levels of teamwork to ensure smooth transmission – the director, producer, floor-manager, sound and lighting engineers all have to know exactly what others are doing so that they can work effectively.

DEFINING A TEAM

A team has:

- *a clear purpose*
- *clear, shared aims*
- *clear sense of individual roles*
- *strong leadership.*

Team-working with colleagues

Take a moment now to reflect on your work over the last week.

- *Think of the people you have worked with.*
- *Think of your role/s and of their roles.*

Now consider: 'In my dealings with all these people over the last week, to what extent have I been working as part of a group and to what extent have I been working in a team?'

List the group events:

▶

▶

▶

List the team events:

▶

▶

▶

HOW GOOD DO YOU THINK YOU ARE AT BEING A TEAM PLAYER?

Below are some of the key characteristics of team-working:

- ▶ *able to take instructions*
- ▶ *aware of own role*
- ▶ *aware of team's aims*
- ▶ *aware of team's purpose*
- ▶ *able to support team members*
- ▶ *able to contribute fully to the work of the team;*

and of the leader:

- ▶ *able to lead a team*
- ▶ *able to gain the trust, support and respect of team members*

- ▶ *able to make decisions*
- ▶ *able to delegate authority.*

The management writer, R. Meredith Belbin in his famous book
Management Teams: Why They Succeed or Fail, determined
from his research that there were certain key qualities in effective
teams. It makes fascinating reading, but essentially he noted that
successful teams contain:

- ▶ a **co-ordinator**: *chairs effectively, is able to get the most from team members, orchestrates the actions of others*
- ▶ a **doer**: *a reliable person who sees actions through, can be prone to perfectionism*
- ▶ a **thinker**: *a strategist – perhaps better at thinking of applications and implications than actually doing*
- ▶ a **supporter**: *reliable, can always be counted on to be there and do things, likes to create a co-operative atmosphere*
- ▶ a **challenger**: *gets the team thinking about what it's doing, perhaps rather prickly and not easily satisfied.*

Belbin uses different terminology from the above simplification.
He stresses that a team should comprise a number of different
personality traits, as above. If all the team members have the same
traits, or if these different roles are not included in the team, the
team will fail to meet its objectives. Too many people are trying
to do the same thing in the same way, or there are gaps in roles or
insufficient challenge to perform effectively.

Figure 14 outlines the characteristics of Belbin's team roles. Look
through the roles now.

- ▶ *Do you recognize the roles in teams in which you have worked?*
- ▶ *Can you see colleagues here?*
- ▶ *Can you see yourself?*

Belbin has devised a Self-Perception Inventory® which allows
people to undertake a self-assessment of their own team-working

strengths. Perhaps you have undertaken one in the workplace – if not, these copyright self-assessments are available online from the Belbin website (www.belbin.com) for around £30. You are likely to find it intriguing. Some people are surprised by the results whilst others may feel that it confirms what they already suspected but had no impartial evidence for.

Insight

It's important to stress that no one personality type or team role is more important than another. But whilst you don't need to be of a certain personality *type* to be an effective team member, being able to work as *part* of a team is crucial, even if you are not the captain.

Roles and descriptions	Team-role contribution	Allowable weaknesses
Plant	Creative, imaginative, unorthodox. Solves difficult problems.	Ignores details. Too preoccupied to communicate effectively.
Resource investigator	Extrovert, enthusiastic, communicative. Explores opportunities. Develops contacts.	Over-optimistic. Loses interest once initial enthusiasm has passed.
Co-ordinator	Mature, confident, a good chairperson. Clarifies goals, promotes decision-making. Delegates well.	Can be seen as manipulative. Delegates personal work.
Shaper	Challenging, dynamic, thrives on pressure. Has the drive and courage to overcome obstacles.	Can provoke others. Hurts people's feelings.

Roles and descriptions	Team-role contribution	Allowable weaknesses
Monitor-evaluator	Sober, strategic and discerning. Sees all the options. Judges accurately.	Lacks drive and the ability to inspire others.
Team-worker	Co-operative, mild, perceptive and diplomatic. Listens, builds, averts friction, calms the waters.	Indecisive in crunch situations. Can be easily influenced.
Implementer	Disciplined, reliable, conservative and efficient. Turns ideas into practical actions.	Somewhat inflexible. Slow to respond to new possibilities.
Completer	Painstaking, conscientious, anxious. Searches out errors and omissions. Delivers on time.	Inclined to worry unduly. Reluctant to delegate. Can be a nit-picker.
Specialist	Single-minded, self-sharing, dedicated. Provides knowledge and skills in rare supply.	Contributes on only a narrow front. Dwells on technicalities. Overlooks the 'big picture'.

Figure 14 Belbin's revised team roles.

Insight

One group of doctoral students on a team-working course was initially perplexed why employers sought these skills. Rapidly convinced of their desirability, some students had difficulty identifying where or how they might have gained such experiences. Listing their sports teams, clubs, societies and part-time work experience, they suddenly realized that all these experiences provided ample evidence of their team-working abilities, transferable to the workplace.

Seizing opportunities to enhance your skills

Whatever your line of work, there will be opportunities to enhance your employability skills. Remember that these are skills which have a value to your current employment as well as to yourself, so seeking to enhance them will also benefit your current employer. You don't necessarily have to look too far – remember that in many aspects of our working life there are positive opportunities and challenges masquerading as insurmountable problems!

OPPORTUNITIES YOU CAN SEIZE TO DEVELOP YOUR SKILL-SET:

Opportunity	Gain
Attending meetings	Discussion/debating/chairing skills
Making a presentation (e.g. to colleagues)	Verbal skills
Taking minutes of meetings	Writing skills
Writing reports	Writing skills
IT skills	Computer literacy/expertise
Organizing an event	Organizational/budgeting skills
Team membership	Team-work skills
Team management	Management/leadership skills
Training a colleague	Training/mentoring skills

The table above is only a short list of possibilities. There will certainly be others which you can identify in the gaps.

CONTRIBUTING TO MEETINGS

Let's consider how you might develop your skills in just one field – for example, contributing to meetings. Most people will attend meetings in some capacity or other, whether in the workplace, as the occasional part of a club or society or some other social gathering (e.g. place of worship). Here is a checklist of some of the points you might ask yourself about your contributions to meetings:

When making my contributions to meetings:	Yes [✓]	No [✗]

Do I listen carefully to the contributions of others?
Do I speak up when I have something to say?
Can other people hear my voice?
Do I make eye contact with people?
Do I leave a meeting wishing I had made a point?
Do I feel that I have explained the point/s clearly?
Do I help to create a constructive atmosphere?
Do I offer support to others?
Do I talk too much?
Do others' eyes roll when I start to speak?
Do I use appropriate body language to reinforce my point?
Do I find myself lost for words or tongue-tied?
Do others comment on my performance?
Do I feel myself blushing?
Do I feel confident about making contributions?
Am I easily influenced or swayed by others?

If I am chairing meetings:	Yes [✓]	No [✗]

Do I ensure that the right people are there?
Do I keep to the agenda?
Do I have a clear agenda and purpose?
Do I indicate the likely finishing time?
Do I create an atmosphere where people can participate?

(Contd)

If I am chairing meetings:	Yes [✓]	No [✗]
Do I encourage people to participate?		
Do I keep fair but firm control of proceedings?		
Do I listen carefully to others?		
Do I make 'listening noises' to show that I'm listening?		
Do I periodically summarize so that everyone understands?		
Do I ensure that decisions are reached fairly?		
Do I ensure that decisions are recorded clearly?		
Do I ensure that anyone absent is informed of decisions?		
If I have a meetings secretary, do I ensure that s/he understands her/his role?		

You can also devise similar checklists for other tasks and activities in which you might be regularly involved.

As a case study, let's take organizing an event. It need not be a large event, perhaps just a small one. There are a number of key questions to ask yourself, as set out in the table.

What is the event?	What is the title and purpose?
	How will people know if they are involved/invited?
	What are the aims?
	How will I know if they have been achieved?
	Have I thought it through from the delegates' perspective or just from mine?
Who is it for?	Who is the target audience?
	Have I taken into account delegates' needs? What about timing, what about disabled access?

Who will I work with?	Am I working solo or is there assistance?
	How will we agree who is responsible for what?
	Do I need to liaise with presenters/speakers/exhibitors?
Where will it take place?	How do I book venue/accommodation?
	Is there a cost and from which budget does this come?
When will it take place?	Have I checked that there are no clashes?
	What is the most convenient time for all concerned?
	Decide date, time, duration – and let everyone know.
How much will it cost?	Are there costs for materials?
What else do I need to arrange?	e.g. Publicity; organizing data projector/laptop; refreshments
Are there any post-event tasks?	e.g. Letters of thanks
How do I plan the activity?	Wall chart? Gantt chart? Sheets of A3 paper? Write in key milestones, mark a weekly countdown, check progress regularly, keep records of correspondence and agreements etc.

Mentoring

In Greek mythology Mentor was a friend of Odysseus and the tutor of Telemachus. His name became synonymous with being a trusted and wise adviser. The term 'mentoring' has evolved to mean where an experienced person (the mentor) shares, guides and provides feedback to a less experienced person (the mentee).

Those with a Classical education will by now be grinding their teeth about the way in which these terms have evolved and become used, but the concept remains helpful.

Insight

It is also worth remembering that the most successful mentors encourage their mentees to develop by encouraging them to reflect on progress and work towards their own solutions. Mentoring does not mean telling the mentee what to do!

FINDING A MENTOR

How can mentoring help you? If you are considering a career move or indeed a completely different type of work, it can be helpful to have someone to guide you. We'll look at this in more detail later but your mentor might be:

▶ *someone already working in your chosen field*
▶ *someone with an overall, if not specific, understanding of the sector*
▶ *a business champion (from a business development agency) who can keep an eye on your progress*
▶ *a friend, preferably a 'critical friend' who will offer constructive advice – which may include asking some awkward questions.*

Work at finding a mentor from whatever source is best. Try trade or professional circles and associations, attend conferences or trade fairs to get a feel for the sector you are trying to enter, use your free local business support service (see the reference section for details), keep your eye open in local or regional papers for events which may give you a flavour of the work and provide networking opportunities.

BEING A MENTOR

It may also be that you can act as a mentor to someone in your current role. This can be extremely useful in helping you define what you do, and how and why you might do it in particular ways.

Indeed, mentors generally learn a lot from their mentees' questions – why, indeed, has it become practice to carry out a task in this way or sequence; are our systems there primarily to help us or our customers; why has no one questioned that practice before? You may find that being a mentor in this capacity actually opens your eyes to your own job and alternative ways of approaching it. Such an experience and process may help you towards the answer you are seeking; maybe it will clarify that you do want to get out and more quickly than you had thought; perhaps it will encourage you to take a different angle in your current post and if that does not fulfil you, then at least you know that you have tried every angle and it really is time to move on. Best of all, the mentoring experience will have cost you nothing but time.

Case studies

JANE RECOGNIZES HER POTENTIAL

Jane has now attended both of her in-service training courses on using computers and some of her college courses on running a business. She no longer feels over-awed by computers and this has given her self-confidence a tremendous lift. She feels excited about the prospect of running a business and feels that she is temperamentally suited to many aspects of the work.

Several of her colleagues have commented on her new enthusiasm and even the Head has noted the spring in her step. Jane knows that there are still many obstacles to overcome and her natural caution is proving an asset here. At least she knows that she doesn't have to make a decision in a hurry.

FRANCIS HAS TAKEN THE PLUNGE

Likewise, Francis has now attended his assertiveness-training course. He was dreading it as the time approached and was longing for a heavy cold or something to prevent him attending. But his wife would have none of it and packed him off, delivering him to the door. Francis found it emotionally draining with role-plays and self-evaluation but also uplifting and fulfilling. He felt he learnt more in that weekend than in all his previous courses at work. It was money well spent. Indeed, his wife could not believe how exhilarated he was.

The first meeting of his working party went superbly and he was impressed with the way in which he presented his views confidently and fluently. He overheard several colleagues say 'Never knew he had it in him'. His growing self-confidence means that he has a new attitude to his work and is ready to consider all future possibilities in a positive light.

RAMISH MAKES PROGRESS

Delighted to have had his suggestion for an article accepted, Ramish has thrown himself into writing it. He has also now attended several meetings of the GP surgery's Patients' Panel and has been pleasantly surprised at the ground-swell of support he has detected for complementary medicine. As this was not initiated by him, he feels that there is genuine support for such provision. One of the GPs appears particularly well-disposed towards the concept and Ramish has had several further discussions with her. Nothing concrete yet, but at least it's encouraging.

In the meantime, Ramish has a new lease of life for his job and sees it now in a different way, focusing on what can be achieved through 'complementary' medicine. The difference is subtle but Ramish senses that his traditional medical colleagues are now more prepared to discuss issues with him rather than regarding him as slightly odd. The weekend conference on complementary medicine he attended provided some stimulating discussion and useful contacts. Certainly, his partner Mia is delighted with the progress made by Ramish both professionally and personally.

THINGS TO REMEMBER

We have considered:

▶ *The importance of communication skills.*

▶ *The importance of team-work skills.*

▶ *Ways you can enhance your skill-set.*

▶ *Being proactive in developing your skills.*

▶ *How being mentored or mentoring someone else can help you.*

ACTION POINTS

▶ *Identify skills which you need to enhance.*

▶ *Identify specific ways in which you can enhance these in your current employment.*

▶ *Identify ways in which you can enhance them outside of work (e.g. by taking on a role in a club to which you belong).*

7

Assessing your attitude to life

In this chapter you will learn:
- *how to gauge your own attitude to life*
- *about the aspects of working life you value*
- *about the key decisions to take for your future*

Recognizing yourself

By now you should be gaining a much clearer idea of your own values and aspirations – in other words the 'Where am I now?' and 'Where do I want to be?' questions. Don't worry if they are not yet all crystal clear – such a process takes time and only by reflecting upon your experiences, strengths, areas for development, worries and concerns are you able to move forward into identifying what is right for you. Remember that you are making a decision about 'me plc' and you will never make more important decisions.

Let us start this chapter by briefly summarizing where you have reached so far. You have considered:

- ▸ *what has made you what you are*
- ▸ *what has made you who you are*
- ▸ *your life-map*
- ▸ *your needs and desires*
- ▸ *your SWOT analysis*
- ▸ *your PEST analysis*
- ▸ *your areas for development in terms of skills.*

As Cardinal Newman is alleged to have observed, 'The only evidence of life is growth' and you are now on that journey of personal growth by starting to recognize and respond to the issues above. Let's continue that journey.

Identifying your personal values

In the box below are some statements about your attitude to life for you to consider. Of course, there are no 'correct' answers but there should be a pattern which emerges with what is appropriate for you.

What is important to me in life

From the following values, tick the ten most important ones for you.

- ▶ *Personal integrity* ☐
- ▶ *Exerting power and influence* ☐
- ▶ *Personal space/time to myself* ☐
- ▶ *Being competitive* ☐
- ▶ *Family/loved ones* ☐
- ▶ *Physical and mental health* ☐
- ▶ *Spiritual fulfilment* ☐
- ▶ *Creativity* ☐
- ▶ *Holidays* ☐
- ▶ *A sense of helping/providing a service to others* ☐
- ▶ *Personal sense of success* ☐
- ▶ *Winning* ☐
- ▶ *Fulfilling work* ☐
- ▶ *Close friends* ☐

From the ten which you have selected, draw cartoons of the five most crucial ones to you in the box provided. You don't have to be an artist – but just use your imagination to depict the ones of most importance to you. For example, if you include holidays you might draw your favourite resort; if it is physical and mental health you might draw someone running etc.

KNOWING HOW YOU WOULD LIKE TO SPEND YOUR TIME IN WORK

From the elements of work listed in the box below, select those ten which you most enjoy (or with some justification, think that you would enjoy). Tick in the appropriate spaces below.

- ▶ *Providing strategic/corporate leadership* ☐
- ▶ *Influencing change* ☐
- ▶ *Increasing efficiency and cost-effectiveness* ☐
- ▶ *Strategic planning* ☐
- ▶ *'Hands-on' involvement* ☐
- ▶ *Analysing numbers/accounting* ☐
- ▶ *Meeting deadlines* ☐
- ▶ *Being creative/innovative* ☐
- ▶ *Negotiating with clients/suppliers* ☐
- ▶ *Project management* ☐
- ▶ *Developing people* ☐
- ▶ *Facilitating teams* ☐
- ▶ *'Making a difference'* ☐
- ▶ *Managing change* ☐

Again, picture yourself in this type of work. If it is analysing numbers, you might show a calculator, if it is problem-solving you might draw a big question mark then put a line through it etc.

CHOOSING THE WORKING ATMOSPHERE YOU WOULD LIKE

Having identified the sphere or nature of work which you find most attractive, how do you foresee the favoured working conditions? Irrespective of whether your preferred employment is with a huge multinational conglomerate, a small or medium-sized enterprise (SME) or a one-person band, what sort of working environment do you favour? Here, we do not mean, for example, a non-smoking environment, but in terms of the overall working relationships and atmosphere. Put a tick in the appropriate spaces below.

- ▶ *Enough time to do what I need to do* ☐
- ▶ *No unnecessary stress* ☐
- ▶ *Meeting challenges* ☐
- ▶ *Feeling able to decline extra work* ☐
- ▶ *Not over-working* ☐
- ▶ *Regular feedback from my line-manager* ☐
- ▶ *Clear lines of communication* ☐
- ▶ *Good relationships with my 'superiors'* ☐
- ▶ *Good relationships with my peers* ☐
- ▶ *Good relationships with my 'subordinates'* ☐
- ▶ *Support for my endeavours* ☐
- ▶ *Feeling valued* ☐
- ▶ *A sense of excitement and flowing adrenaline* ☐
- ▶ *Corporate goals/mission clearly understood* ☐
- ▶ *Able to delegate appropriately to others* ☐

Again, draw a representation of the five characteristics you would most value. For example, if it is clear lines of communication, simply draw some arrowed lines; if it is good relationships with peers, draw three smiling faces on the same level.

What is your attitude to life?

How do your friends describe you? As a realist, an optimist, a pessimist or a cynic? They may not necessarily know the 'real' you but others' views can be accurate. More importantly, if your proposed future life involves an element of risk, you need to be of a particular disposition. If your anticipated future career is as a self-employed underwater tap-dancer, you would need certain qualities and attributes: the ability to swim and dive, the ability to look aesthetic in your actions, to have powerful lungs and all-round fitness. But on top of this you would need to be an optimist that your endeavours would succeed in attracting a sufficiently large audience and to be a risk-taker, not only physically but also financially. If you are temperamentally ultra-cautious, then no matter what your ambition is, you should forget the project. It just wouldn't work for you.

Insight
Clearly, the example is absurd, but sometimes we may be blind to certain characteristics which we have and ignore the way in which others can see them.

Are you a toll-booth attendant?

In other words, are you willing to accept change?

Establishing your own outlook on life is vital in thinking about which direction to take for the future. Let's carry out a few activities to demonstrate this.

ACTIVITY 1

Look at the following well-known proverbs. Indicate whether you agree or disagree with these:

		Yes	No
1	You can't have the penny and the bun.	☐	☐
2	What you gain on the swings, you lose on the roundabouts.	☐	☐
3	God helps those who help themselves.	☐	☐
4	All's well that ends well.	☐	☐
5	Don't count your chickens before they're hatched.	☐	☐
6	You learn something new every day.	☐	☐

ACTIVITY 2

Look at the pairs of well-known proverbs and phrases below. Tick the one which is more in tune with your philosophy or outlook on life.

1	You're never too old to learn.	☐
2	You can't teach an old dog new tricks.	☐
3	No smoke without fire.	☐
4	Every cloud has a silver lining.	☐
5	If something can go wrong, it will.	☐
6	It'll be alright on the night.	☐
7	Many hands make light work.	☐

(Contd)

8 Too many cooks spoil the broth. ☐
9 Look before you leap. ☐
10 Nothing ventured, nothing gained. ☐

ACTIVITY 3

Look at Figure 15. What do you see?

Figure 15

ASSESSING YOUR ANSWERS

What were your responses to these activities?

▶ Activity 1: *Proverbs 3, 4 and 6 are optimistic, whilst 1, 2 and 5 are pessimistic.*
▶ Activity 2: *Proverbs 1, 4, 6, 7 and 10 are optimistic, whilst 2, 3, 5, 8 and 9 are pessimistic.*
▶ Activity 3: *To you, was the bottle half-full or half-empty?*

If you erred towards the more pessimistic interpretations of the above, then maybe you are by nature a pessimist or cynic. If you erred towards the optimistic, then that is likely to be your disposition.

Are you an optimist or pessimist?

An optimistic person is usually able to deal with disappointment more
easily and to bounce back from the trials of life, whereas the pessimist
may give up rather too easily and imagine difficulties where there
aren't any. Of course, there can be a danger in being falsely optimistic,
of not seeing the dangers, problems or difficulties which may lie ahead
(just like our underwater tap-dancer earlier). It is often said that the
difference between Shakespeare's comedies and his tragedies is not so
much in the plot but rather in the disposition of the characters to deal
with the adversity they face. In the comedies, the main characters have
sufficient strength of character to turn potential misfortune to their
advantage, whereas in the tragedies they become overwhelmed by the
situations with which they are faced, which become insuperable with
the 'tragic flaw' in the character's personality.

Personality

Is it possible to 'measure' an individual's personality? Certainly,
we can identify specific personality traits, but ultimately each
individual's personality is unique. One of the best-known personality
tests is the Myers-Briggs Type Indicator®. This is a self-report

questionnaire based on the theory of psychological type developed
by Carl Jung. The questionnaire was developed by Katherine Cook
Briggs and Isabel Briggs Myers and, worldwide, over 3.5 million
such indicators are undertaken annually. In essence, it identifies
individuals' preferred responses in a range of situations, dividing
people into extroverts and introverts. It's important to recognize
what these terms mean – it is more sophisticated than the commonly
held belief that introverts are shy and extroverts are outgoing.

What is crucially important also is that the test does not suggest
that particular personality types are 'better' than others. To do so
would simply suggest that there is a desired template we should all
strive for and that is nonsense. But it is helpful to know the general
way in which we are likely to respond to certain situations – the
areas in which we feel comfortable (our 'comfort zone') and those
we may prefer to avoid or in which we lack confidence. People
who have undertaken such questionnaires generally comment on
the extraordinary level of accuracy of the results and how they
have helped them to understand their workplace behaviour.
A range of websites for accessing such personality tests is listed
in the reference section.

Knowing what suits you

Figure 16 is a list of the factors which you may have to consider.
You will notice that the term 'security' is missing from the list –
it may be more apparent in some work than others but, as this
book has shown, it can be illusory. There is no one set of desirable
responses here – rather, it is a question of the working style and
ethos which best suits your personality. However, you should ask
yourself some basic questions:

ASSESSING WHAT SUITS YOU

▶ *If a set routine, a known and regular income and being able to
take for-granted all the infrastructure of a large organization*

is important to you, would you be able to work for a small
organization where a variety of roles are expected, or work for
yourself?
- ▶ *If your list comprises mostly negative factors, where will a*
  more positive working environment be found?
- ▶ *If your current work offers a mixture of positive and negative*
  factors, can you identify which ones you could take with you
  and which ones you would be happy to leave behind?

PSYCHOMETRIC TESTING

An extension of such reflection is **psychometric testing**. This involves
interpreting your response to a battery of multiple-choice questions
relating to your work and social outlook. It is based on the premise
that people are suited to different occupations and occupational
sectors according to their psychological make-up. Furthermore,
that given certain responses, some people should avoid specific
occupations! A number of these tests are based on Jungian
principles (like the Myers-Briggs Type Indicator®). Some companies
use psychometric testing as part of their recruitment process,
particularly if the job involves selling to the public. For example,
in the UK Honda uses the 'Discus Phrase-based Questionnaire'.

	Factors present in current work	Factors I wish to retain	Factors I wish to reject
Regular income			
Opportunity to enhance basic income			
Paid holidays			
Sick pay			
Company car			
Sense of fulfilment			
Externally imposed deadlines			

(Contd)

	Factors present in current work	Factors I wish to retain	Factors I wish to reject
Pension			
Welfare scheme			
Training/development			
Autonomy			
Work at home			
Nights away from home			
Travel (at my discretion)			
Travel (on someone else's instructions)			
Valued colleagues			
Externally imposed discipline			
Self-imposed discipline			
Intellectual/mental stimulation			
Boredom			
Challenge			
Insurmountable difficulties			
Negative stress			
Positive stress			
Infrastructure (secretarial/ IT support etc.)			
Job satisfaction			
Creativity			
Sense of identity in organization			
Sense of self-identity			
Set routine			
Variety			
Clear guidelines			
Red tape			

Figure 16 Assessing what's important to you.

Multiple intelligences

Do you remember the activity you undertook at the beginning of Chapter 2, about positive and negative learning experiences? That illustrated some of the aspects and approaches to learning you valued or which you found difficult. Your response had nothing to do with your 'intelligence'. Indeed, these days, it is recognized that the traditional view of intelligence and measuring it by IQ is very limited and inaccurate. People learn in a wide variety of ways from a multitude of experiences and through a variety of their senses.

The psychologist Howard Gardner recognized this and devised the term 'multiple intelligences'. Gardner identified different intelligences, as illustrated in Figure 17.

Verbal ⎫	These are based on the traditional academic approach to learning.
Mathematical ⎭	
Spatial capacity	The ability shown by artists, architects and others who think in a three-dimensional manner.
Kinaesthetic	Those who learn best by 'doing'.
Musical	Self-explanatory!
Personal intelligences	Interpersonal skills with other people and intrapersonal skills of knowing oneself.

Figure 17 Howard Gardner's 'multiple intelligences'.

Having a sense of how you learn best is clearly helpful. As we are seeing, it has a strong influence on the type of work in which you feel most fulfilled.

Emotional intelligence

Emotional intelligence is a relatively new term, based on the work of the American author, Daniel Goleman and is an extension of the multiple intelligences work of Gardner. There are five components of Emotional Intelligence (sometimes called EI):

▶ **Self-awareness:** *This is exhibited by self-confidence, realistic self-assessment and a self-deprecating sense of humour.*
▶ **Self-management:** *This is exhibited by trustworthiness and integrity, comfort with ambiguity and openness to change.*
▶ **Self-motivation:** *This is exhibited by a strong desire to achieve, optimism and high organizational commitment.*
▶ **Empathy:** *This is exhibited by expertise in building and retaining talent, cross-cultural sensitivity, and service to client and customers.*
▶ **Social skills:** *This is exhibited by the ability to lead change efforts, persuasiveness, and expertise in building and leading teams.*

Goleman argues that emotional intelligence is particularly relevant in jobs requiring a high degree of social interaction.

In essence, many of the activities you have undertaken whilst reading this book have been covered by the above aspects. Certainly, you will have a higher degree of self-awareness; and in making your choices you are displaying self-management, based upon a greater understanding of what motivates you. The activities in developing your transferable skills have focused on social, team and influencing skills and towards sensitivity to others as well as yourself.

Checking the lifeboat

By now you are beginning to get a feel for what best suits you. You need to take into account a number of factors:

- ▶ *your temperament*
- ▶ *your aspirations*
- ▶ *your skills*
- ▶ *your experience*
- ▶ *your qualities*
- ▶ *your individual situation.*

However, as we have seen, life is not always neat and tidy and things don't always fit into place – and that is certainly true today of careers. How many times have we taken a decision in life which has proved to be beneficial – or otherwise? Think back to the life-map you drew in Chapter 3. How many of those major influencing events in your life were subsequently revealed to have been major turning points because of decisions made?

There are times when we have to make uncomfortable decisions about our working life and employment, yet at the same time be comfortable with living with the consequences of those same decisions.

Insight

In consultancy, you are only as good as your last job. Screw something up and word gets around quickly – or so I'm told! Likewise, word gets around quickly about your expertise and you will find referrals come your way from unexpected sources.

If you stay where you are
- ▶ *There may still be uncomfortable times ahead.*
- ▶ *Things may not get better.*
- ▶ *At least it is a known environment and situation.*
- ▶ *'Better the devil you know than the one you don't'.*

If you 'jump'

▶ *Do you know where you are heading?*
▶ *Is it 'out of the frying pan into the fire'?*
▶ *Is it 'a leap in the dark'?*
▶ *Or is it a question of 'jumping ship before it goes down'?*
▶ *Or of jumping before you are pushed?*
▶ *Can you accept an element of risk?*
▶ *What element of risk can you accept?*
▶ *Can you live with the consequences of the decision – good and bad?*

There are all sorts of issues to consider where we may know the background and be able to predict what is happening (particularly if we have carried out a PEST analysis) or where we would be advised to seek the opinion of someone not so caught up in the events as we are. However, as before, try to select someone whose opinion you really value and who will not come up with some of the clichés listed above!

We have seen that life, by its very nature, involves change. Both our attitude to change and our attitude to others are based on our perception of them. In order to genuinely move forward, we have to understand ourselves, our attitude to risk and how far we wish to take control of situations rather than allowing situations or long-standing custom and practice to control us.

Insight

Perhaps, a useful saying to remember is the phrase:

**If you always do what you've always done,
you'll always get what you've always got.**

Anonymous

And if by the time you reach the end of this book, you are genuinely happy with 'what you've always got', that is fine.

Case studies

JANE GAINS A NEW LEASE OF LIFE

Jane has progressed enormously since attending her courses. A new air of enthusiasm pervades all that she does and colleagues and friends have commented on this. She remains level-headed and cautious, knowing that it would be easy to fall into an unrealistic mental state with her new-found enthusiasm. Can she maintain this new zest as a teacher? But she knows that fundamentally the work does not offer her the creativity and sense of being her own boss she craves.

She has considered joining or establishing a co-operative venture for her craft work, knowing that in many cases these work extremely successfully. She has researched the topic carefully, but decided that the joint ownership of every aspect of the business does not appeal to her and that she needs independence. However, Jane knows that she can join the 'supply teacher' list in her area and that this will be a most valuable financial support to her in the early stages. It will not be professionally rewarding, for she knows how supply teachers can be marginalized in schools, but few other jobs offer such a financial lifeline and she is immensely aware of her good fortune here. Currently, Jane is in the fortunate position of having nothing to lose.

FRANCIS RECOGNIZES THE LIMITS

Buoyed up by the decisions he has already taken, Francis now realizes that he needs to operate within a secure framework. It is something which matters deeply to him and he knows that he lacks the self-discipline to go it alone in any venture. But he also realizes that he needs greater autonomy than he has had previously and that his previous working environment, which he had considered the norm, was actually a straitjacket. There were certainly lost opportunities but he hadn't seen them and the culture of the bank had not encouraged any employee to seek them.

But it's no use bewailing those now – Francis must focus on the future. What he's seeking now is something with greater autonomy yet with an externally imposed discipline.

RAMISH IS BANKING ON A NEW FUTURE

Feeling a new lease of life from his recent activities, Ramish now also considers that he is prepared to take both a professional and a financial risk. He researches carefully all the aspects of establishing his own complementary medicine practice – additional market research about likely demand, possible funding sources, appropriate premises within the locality, set-up costs, additional qualifications and professional registrations which he might seek in order to offer a wider range of services and the feasibility of bringing in other professionals.

He has approached his local bank for details of starting his own business and received a helpful starter pack from them. He has also consulted the range of self-help books available to give him better background knowledge.

THINGS TO REMEMBER

We have considered:

▶ *Your attitude to life in general.*

▶ *The aspects of working life you value.*

▶ *How self-knowledge can inform your decisions.*

▶ *The importance of making decisions in a rational, strategic way.*

▶ *Getting ready to build on the new foundations of your self-knowledge.*

ACTION POINTS

▶ *Clarify in your own mind the element of risk you are prepared to accept.*

▶ *Without making elaborate arrangements which nullify the benefit of any decision you make, list the back-up safety nets available (if any).*

8

....

Where are you going next?

In this chapter you will learn:
- *which planning techniques can help you plan your future*
- *how to develop some generic employability skills*
- *about the job application and interview process*
- *about the core elements of satisfying work for you*

Making the most of choices

As we have seen throughout this book, life is about making decisions. With every decision, clearly there are choices. There are choices about lifestyle – not merely the level of income we desire, but the means to achieve that. The style and the nature of the work we are involved with may be as important as the employment or business sector we select. Choices are not only about what we want to do but, just as importantly, what we don't want to do.

> ### Insight
> In aiming for a particular lifestyle you must balance risks against gains – potential benefits against potential drawbacks. You must balance the known (or at least the likely) against the unknown or the unlikely.

By this stage of the book, and your own voyage of self-discovery, you will have a clearer idea about a number of issues:

▶ *your motivations, your aspirations, your fears, your strengths and your weaknesses*

- *the type of lifestyle you are seeking*
- *whether you are aiming for full-time permanent employment, part-time employment, self-employment, a consultancy portfolio or, indeed, no employment of any type.*

You will not be alone in your decision to change – The Office for National Statistics says that 16% of the British workforce, or 3.3 million people, change jobs or work each year. However, unlike the majority of them, you will be different. Because whatever decision you have made will have been based on what you have learnt about yourself; your assessment of the types of skills and knowledge you have to market; your evaluation of the marketplace in which you might operate and the working environment in which you feel you will grow personally and professionally. Consequently, you will not necessarily have to read through all the information below but just that which applies to your chosen destination.

Accessing support networks

If you are already in employment and you are aiming to remain within your current employment sector, you will probably know of the support networks available in your line of work. For example, the Chartered Management Institute (CMI) provides members seeking to enhance their management skills and expertise with CMI's research papers, publications, conferences, industry briefings and a wide range of courses at different levels which can be followed by open-learning or at a local centre, such as a further education college.

SEEKING FURTHER EMPLOYMENT IN A SECTOR IN WHICH YOU HAVE ALREADY WORKED

You can try:

- *professionally linked support in your own sector*
- *professional bodies/societies*
- *trade unions*
- *websites.*

SEEKING A DIFFERENT LINE OF EMPLOYMENT IN ANOTHER SECTOR

You can try:

▶ *that sector's professional bodies*
▶ *professional publications in that sector.*

SEEKING SELF-EMPLOYMENT OR PORTFOLIO EMPLOYMENT

You can try your local:

▶ *Tax Information Centre (TIC)*
▶ *Chamber of Commerce (provides a good opportunity to network)*
▶ *branch of the Federation of Small Businesses*
▶ *further education college*
▶ *business start-up agency.*

A full list of business start-up funding support agencies is offered in the list of contacts in 'Taking it Further' on p. 195. However, depending on where you live, these will include 'one-stop shops' such as:

England:	Business Links
Wales:	Business Eye
Scotland:	Business Gateway
Northern Ireland:	Invest Northern Ireland

Additionally, there are other devolved agencies and many people approach their local enterprise agency. See the further information on p. 195.

SEEKING FURTHER EDUCATION OR TRAINING IN YOUR SPECIALISM

You can try the organizations or view the websites listed in the Useful Addresses section on pp. 192–4.

The chapter now focuses on generic skills necessary for improving your employability.

Managing time

Managing time is a constant source of pressure for many people who feel that they have too many responsibilities for the time available. Some people are better time managers than others – they like to be organized, can prioritize, can project ahead and work backwards by allocating tasks to meet specific deadlines. But, whether you are looking to change employment sector, gain promotion or work for yourself, everyone can gain from better time-management skills. So how do yours rate?

START AT THE BEGINNING

A good starting place for developing your own time management skills is to consider the main tasks in your job/role. This will vary according to whether you are in full- or part-time work, your domestic situation etc. In other words, you need to identify what tasks your work involves. What tasks do you have to get done in order to meet your employment/study/family commitments?

In the box below, list the main tasks of your work. Group them together so that there are a maximum of ten.

1

2

3

4

5

6

7

(Contd)

:   **8**

:   **9**

:   **10**

MATCHING SIZE OF TASK TO IMPORTANCE

The circle below represents the entirety of your work. Using the list of tasks you identified above, allocate each task a segment of the circle according to its importance in your mind for carrying out your work. For example, if you consider that writing up the sales figures of your department is the single most important aspect of your work, you will allocate it the largest segment. (All segments should be as accurate as possible but don't worry about geometrical precision!)

Points to consider:

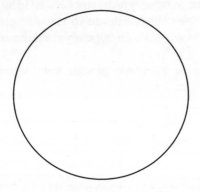

- ▶ *Are there any discrepancies between what you consider to be the most important tasks and the amount of time you spend on them?*
- ▶ *Are there any tasks which you feel rushed or pressurized for time?*
- ▶ *Are there any tasks or responsibilities on which you spend too much time for their overall importance?*

132

Some people are fortunate to have considerable amounts of 'discretionary time'. They can decide what they do when, how and in which sequence – provided that they execute work effectively and meet their and others' deadlines, targets and budgets, they can distribute the motivationally low pay-off tasks among the high pay-off tasks. Others may be less fortunate.

DO I HAVE A TIME MANAGEMENT PROBLEM?

How do you fare in this questionnaire? Read the numbered statements and then rate according to the column headings.

	Very often	Quite often	Sometimes	Rarely or never
1 I can't get on with my work because of interruptions outside my control.				
2 The meetings I attend could be better organized.				
3 Problems I have not foreseen interfere with my work.				
4 Colleagues take my time without making an adequate contribution to my effectiveness.				
5 I waste the time of others with whom I work.				

(Contd)

		Very often	Quite often	Sometimes	Rarely or never
6	I find tasks to keep busy, avoiding things I should be doing.				
7	Poorly designed systems in the organization waste my time.				
8	I keep my work in piles on the desk, on shelves, by the phone etc.				
9	I put off big or difficult jobs.				
10	I waste time looking for files, papers etc.				
11	Meetings take too much of my time.				
12	I have my diary/ organizer with me.				
13	Most of my time is under my control.				
14	I set a priority for each piece of work I do.				

	Very often	Quite often	Sometimes	Rarely or never
15 I organize my workspace/office in a systematic manner.				
16 I list tasks on a 'to do' list to keep my priorities before me.				
17 Decisions and actions are followed up promptly.				
18 I ask myself: 'Am I working on the right thing in the right way at the right time?'				

PROCRASTINATION

Procrastination – or putting things off – is the most commonly indulged-in time-waster. We all do it to a lesser or greater degree. The key point is to be able to identify when and why we are doing it. Procrastinators can be grouped into:

▶ *Doubters – don't believe their ability to do a job/task.*
▶ *Perfectionists – set themselves impossibly high standards then fail to achieve them.*
▶ *Rebels – want to show their control over themselves, others and the situation by constantly fire-fighting and working to last-minute deadlines.*
▶ *Socializers – involve themselves in gossip, extended lunch breaks and constant tea breaks. (Do not confuse this with the perfectly acceptable and healthy use of a break time to relax and refresh your energies for the tasks ahead.)*

Do you recognize any of these factors in yourself? This is well worth asking and being *totally honest* with yourself. If you intend becoming self-employed you really do need to recognize this quality and what you can do about it – otherwise, it will cost you time and, literally, money.

Reasons for procrastination

▶ *You think the task is unpleasant, overwhelming, not fun, outside your 'comfort zone', or a risk.*
▶ *You don't know where or how to start.*
▶ *'There isn't time.'*
▶ *You won't be able to do the job perfectly.*
▶ *You think the job's too big – you can do lots of little jobs in the same time.*

My reasons for procrastinating

```



```

Some ideas for controlling procrastination

1 Recognize that you are doing it:
   ▷ *Are you doing lots of fragmented tasks?*
   ▷ *Are you worrying and fretting – wasting time on 'negative emotions'?*
   ▷ *Look at your list of priorities. Are you really supposed to be doing that small task?*
   ▷ *Should you be discussing the weekend's match?*
   ▷ *Did you really have to take that phone call? Use your voicemail system effectively.*

2 Admit that you have been wasting time:
   ▷ *Adopt a positive attitude – think of a worse situation.*
   ▷ *Decide to face the task square on and take control.*

> *Think back to the main objectives of your work.*
> *Think through previous jobs or tasks to recognize that fears of failure are usually unfounded.*

3 Method

> *Find an appropriate place for the task – does everything have to be done from the same base?*
> *Don't 'file' it away – clear your desk to make it the only task.*
> *Decide to do the most unpleasant task of the day first – after that, things can only get better!*
> *Or, get into the swing of the working day by 'warming up' on a small but important task first (but make sure you progress to the main task soon).*
> *Break the task down into manageable chunks.*
> *Commit yourself to the task by telling someone you're going to do it.*
> *Set yourself a deadline.*
> *Reward yourself at stages throughout the job – but not every five minutes!*
> *Remove distractions.*
> *Do one job at a time.*

Activity for procrastination

Now think of times when you have procrastinated. Ask yourself the following questions:

What was the task?

Why didn't I want to start?

What did I do instead?

What was my excuse for not starting?

What were the consequences?

(Contd)

In general:

What types of task do I put off?

What are my favourite excuses?

How can I recognize when it happens again?

Some suggestions to help with procrastination
Completing the table below will help you to identify ways of
dealing with time wasting and procrastination.

Time waster	Possible causes	Ways to overcome	My improvement plan
Taking phone call after phone call	'Politeness'	Use voicemail/ answering machine to screen calls	Switch on voicemail when I have important tasks to do
Email	Feel I have to reply as soon as mail comes in	Prioritize responses	Reply in batches

Time waster	Possible causes	Ways to overcome	My improvement plan

PRIORITIZING

At the start of any given day, make a written list of the tasks facing you – this is always good practice for your diary anyway. Think of all those tasks as an archer's target, as shown in Figure 18.

Divide your tasks into three categories:

▶ *Tasks which you **must** do (**M**). These are important, urgent and non-negotiable tasks. Failing to complete them will cause major inconvenience for yourself, colleagues, customers or suppliers. There is no way you can avoid these tasks.*
▶ *Tasks which you **should** do (**S**). These are less important and less urgent than those at the centre of the target. You can delay these until you have the M tasks completed. However, if you delay them too long, they will simply become 'must do' tasks.*

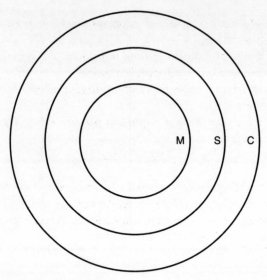

Figure 18 The must, should and could do target.

> *Plan ahead and aim to complete (or at least make a start) on
> these before they become urgent.*
> ▶ *Tasks which you **could** do (**C**). These are currently unimportant
> and time devoted to them will only detract from completing
> other more important tasks. Indeed, you might ask yourself
> 'What would be the consequence of not doing this task?' If
> there is no significant problem, why do it anyway?*

Don't fool yourself that there is nothing which you can omit or which
is less important than others. If some tasks are more important, it
follows that others are less important. In recognizing this, you are
prioritizing and are on your way to managing your time.

The ability to separate urgency and importance is vital to effective
time management. The following matrix is useful to distinguish
between tasks, as follows:

Urgent and important	**Urgent** but not important
Important but not urgent	Neither important nor urgent

- *Tasks which are* **'urgent and important'** *need your immediate and full attention.*
- *Those which are* **'urgent** *but not important' need immediate attention but could be dispatched quickly.*
- *Those which are* **'important** *but not urgent' need addressing fully in time.*
- *Those which are 'neither important nor urgent' – why are you even considering doing them?*

Insight

Aim for 'twofer' tasks – 'two tasks for the price of one'. How about shredding old documents whilst you are waiting for the printer to generate something new or whilst waiting for that promised phone call to be returned?

Activity

Identify a 'normal' working day for yourself. Allocate the various tasks you undertake to the different parts of the matrix in Figure 19. What can you learn from this?

Urgent and important	**Urgent** but not important
Important but not urgent	Neither important nor urgent

Figure 19 Matrix template for self-completion.

The 4Ds alternative approach

An alternative to the above approach is the 4Ds. Make a list of all the things you have to do. Then put them into the appropriate boxes in Figure 20.

Do	Delegate
Delay	Dump

Figure 20 4Ds matrix template for self-completion.

▶ *The list in the **do** box should get smaller as you get better at time management.*
▶ **Delegate** *where you can (or dump and see how important it was).*
▶ *Use the **delay** box to park things briefly while you deal with the do box – but don't let it get urgent!*
▶ **Dump** *trivial things even if you want to do them.*

REDUCING TASKS TO A MANAGEABLE SIZE

Strategies for enhancing your time management should include focusing on breaking down a large task into its smaller component chunks. Such 'chunking' allows the task to be more manageable. There are two ways of doing this: (1) pizza slicing and (2) nibbling.

Pizza slicing

As shown in Figure 21, this approach goes right to the heart of the problem, undertaking a manageable chunk at a time. You might liken this approach to some aspects of gardening. You identify

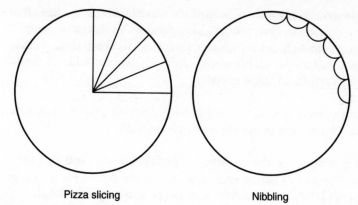

Pizza slicing   Nibbling

Figure 21 Pizza slicing and nibbling, to reduce tasks to a manageable size.

a part of the garden that needs attention and then do everything in that area: cutting back undergrowth, weeding, digging the soil over, replanting etc. The rest of the garden needs doing but you've made a substantial impact in that one area.

Nibbling

As the name suggests, this involves taking small, bite-sized chunks at a time, gradually reducing the size of the task. You might liken this approach to the way that many people approach home decoration: collect colour charts, then decide on a colour scheme, then buy the paint, then buy the brushes, then do the preparation, and finally do the decoration once all the background work is done and it seems manageable.

Managing stress

Stress is basically a demand made on the adaptive capacities of the mind and body. Traditionally, stress was viewed as a bad thing, to be avoided or reduced. However, this assumes that all stress is bad, which is an over-simplification. All athletes, sports people, actors or presenters will tell you that they cannot perform at their best unless they feel *some* stress. Literally, they need to feel the rush of adrenalin in order to achieve. If you have looked at the BBC *Raise Your Game* website you will have noticed this. Likewise, many people need challenges which excite them and keep them on their toes, without which life would ultimately become dull. All these are examples of 'good stress'.

Obviously, there is also 'bad stress' – demands placed on us which we cannot meet physically or psychologically.

It is useful to be able to differentiate these, as they will vary for each person. What causes bad stress for one person can be a source of exhilaration for another. It might be useful just to identify this and, if appropriate, discuss it with a friend or colleague – or particularly with someone working in the employment sector you may be thinking of joining. You can note down your thoughts on stress in the following box.

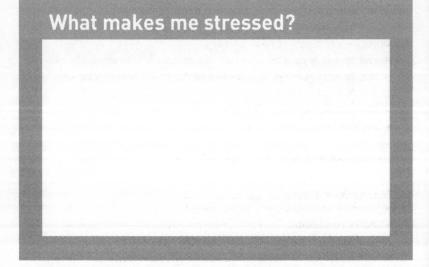

What makes me stressed?

There is certainly a proven link between stress and coronary heart-disease (CHD). Dr Eric Brunner and his colleagues at University College, London conducted a longitudinal study over 20 years (*The Whitehall II study*) on the incidence of CHD in civil servants.

Contributory factors of CHD include smoking, excessive drinking, serum cholesterol level, family history and the level of fibrinogen (a blood-clotting agent). It had often been thought that workers with the highest level of managerial and decision-making responsibility would be those most at risk of stress, as measured by the incidence of CHD.

However, they discovered that in their civil servants, as the level of job control rose so the level of fibrinogen fell. The effect was almost as large as the effect of not smoking or drinking. Furthermore, with an increase in job control, there was a rise in motivation and a reduction in absenteeism. Certainly, it is well-established that absentee rates among the self-employed (who are likely to have substantial control over their work) are amongst the lowest.

Medical experts also categorize two particular 'types' as being at risk of CHD. Type A is characterized by:

▶ *a chronic sense of time urgency*
▶ *free-floating hostility*
▶ *easily aroused anger, irritation and impatience over minor matters*
▶ *competitive and hard-driving*
▶ *inflexible.*

Type B is less stressed than Type A but is characterized by:

▶ *over-achievers*
▶ *set high standards/are perfectionists*
▶ *often to be found in the 'caring professions' (e.g. teaching and health-care)*
▶ *expect others to achieve the same high standards as themselves.*

Of course, stress is not always externally imposed. People who are high-achievers often impose extremely high expectations on themselves, making themselves their own worst enemies. Is it appropriate at times to be gentler on yourself and to take more note of what you value overall in life? What are the ways in which you might be able to remove or reduce some of the negative aspects of stress?

Some employers also offer stress counselling or stress management courses. Check with your staff development office, if you have one. Some courses may be available anonymously or out of hours so that your line manager does not have to countersign your application form or agree to your attending. This can be advantageous because it may be the line manager who is causing some of the stress!

An additional source of support or advice may be your home insurance company. Many companies now have a confidential helpline which you can access 24 hours a day for advice about stress management or health-care. Check your policy for details. Additionally, many trade unions and professional associations also provide such a service for their members. Again, check your membership pack for details.

Marketing yourself

The term marketing does not just mean selling. Yes, of course you will be selling yourself through your services, expertise or experience, perhaps to the highest bidder. But marketing is much more sophisticated than that. It involves:

▶ *researching carefully your potential market/s*
▶ *establishing what your product/service portfolio is*
▶ *establishing a specific benefit (in quality, range, speed of service, flexibility etc.) which no competitor can offer – your* unique selling proposition (USP)
▶ *establishing a specific market where what you offer is of clear value and worth.*

This would be equally true whether your market is as an employee targeting an employer or as a consultant marketing his/her services. Yet the highest bidder is not necessarily the most appropriate home for your services. Before you commit yourself to one purchaser, whether it be as an employee or as a freelance or business, you would be wise to establish some 'rules of engagement'. Depending on whether you are approaching someone as an employee, as a consultant or trader, you will wish to find out what the purchaser has on offer. These would include the following.

If considering employment:

▶ *Apart from income, what else can the employer offer me?*
▶ *What about professional or personal development?*
▶ *What about encouragement to pursue qualifications or gain additional experience?*
▶ *What amount of autonomy will I be allowed in the post?*
▶ *How much scope is there for independent thought or actions?*
▶ *Where can I aim for in the future?*
▶ *What if the company/organization contracts: how will I continue to gain the employability skills I've been developing through this book?*

If considering self-employment:

Perhaps you have decided on *self-employment* or to *start a business*. As you develop your product or service portfolio, you may gain a deal with a particular customer:

▶ *Is it a once-only deal?*
▶ *Is there the opportunity for repeat business?*
▶ *Is there scope for you to offer similar, related products or services so that the purchaser might buy a complete package?*
▶ *What facilities, services or opportunities can the purchaser provide for you which might make the work easier, more pleasant, more stimulating or reliable?*

- ▶ *What level of expenses will the purchaser provide or are you expected to pick up the tab for all of these?*
- ▶ *On what basis will the purchaser be paying? Weekly, monthly, after each 'delivery'?*
- ▶ *What time lag is there between delivery and payment – instant, at the end of the month, after two months?*

Insight

Being a consultant requires you to work both independently and interdependently. Some clients will take an interest in your other work, regarding it as enriching the work you do with them. Others couldn't give a hoot – as long as you deliver their needs, nothing else and no one else matters. If you can't live with this, don't become a consultant.

Maintaining your employability

Having read this book, at the back of your mind should always be the question '*How do I maintain my employability?*' You will be only too aware by now that having certain skills and knowledge at one moment in time does not mean that such skills will always be sought. Knowledge and skills can atrophy and die and one must be constantly conscious of changing needs and demands, retaining flexibility and adaptability.

FORCE FIELD ANALYSIS

The famous American sociologist Kurt Lewin developed a planning tool called Force Field Analysis. This was designed as a tool for organizations planning change and needing to identify the forces which would make it happen (*driving forces*) and also the *restraining forces*. In Figure 22 you can also see that the size and boldness of the arrows indicates their strength. In this case it represents how an individual might respond to the challenge of starting up a business.

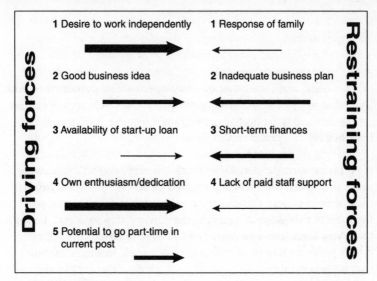

Driving forces	Restraining forces
1 Desire to work independently	1 Response of family
2 Good business idea	2 Inadequate business plan
3 Availability of start-up loan	3 Short-term finances
4 Own enthusiasm/dedication	4 Lack of paid staff support
5 Potential to go part-time in current post	

Figure 22 Example of a force field analysis.

In general, managers who use the force-field analysis tool or those planning change would need to examine how they can capitalize on the driving forces (e.g. encouraging support, celebrating the desired behaviours and performance), as well as identifying how to deal with the restraining forces (e.g. isolating potentially negative forces or seeking to influence by open debate any powerful detractors). The bigger the arrow, the more powerful the force is.

You can also use this technique successfully to develop your own plans (as in the example shown in Figure 22).

Insight

Whatever the situation – as an employee or as a business – stay in touch with developments, predict the trends, gain the skills and knowledge and be able to market your flexibility and adaptability where others get left behind.

Seize the day

A useful Latin tag to remember is '*Carpe Diem*' – 'Seize the day'. In other words, make the most of every opportunity presented to you. Indeed, don't just respond to opportunities, actively seek them out on the basis that, as humans, we are not just the products of our lives but are the producers of them.

If you have seen the film *Dead Poets' Society*, you will remember that the teacher John Keating (played by Robin Williams) exhorts his pupils to follow this dictum – to become self-aware and push themselves to the limits 'to make their lives extraordinary'. Despite the tragic suicide of one pupil (whose over-zealous, controlling father prevents him from following his artistic leanings, insisting that he becomes a doctor instead), the abiding memory of the film is that most of the youngsters have awoken their self-awareness and will actively seek life-enhancing opportunities.

Insight
As Theodore Roosevelt is credited with saying: 'In any moment of decision the best thing you can do is the right thing, the next best thing is the wrong thing, and the worst thing you can do is nothing.'

We will now look at possible ways forward to improving your employability, in particular, applying for jobs.

Applying for jobs

Assuming that you wish to gain an employed post with an organization, the most common way of achieving that still remains the job application. This process is divided into a number of stages which are given in the following flowchart in Figure 23.

This sequence holds true for most organizations although there may be some differences about, for example, whether candidates are interviewed on the same day or over a period of time and when references are taken up. Some organizations do this after the interview so that they are not swayed in interview by someone else's opinion. In essence, within the UK, it is common for public sector jobs to be interviewed on the same day, but much less common in the private sector or through agencies.

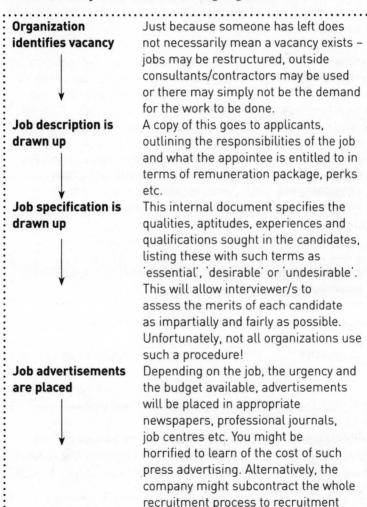

Organization identifies vacancy	Just because someone has left does not necessarily mean a vacancy exists – jobs may be restructured, outside consultants/contractors may be used or there may simply not be the demand for the work to be done.
Job description is drawn up	A copy of this goes to applicants, outlining the responsibilities of the job and what the appointee is entitled to in terms of remuneration package, perks etc.
Job specification is drawn up	This internal document specifies the qualities, aptitudes, experiences and qualifications sought in the candidates, listing these with such terms as 'essential', 'desirable' or 'undesirable'. This will allow interviewer/s to assess the merits of each candidate as impartially and fairly as possible. Unfortunately, not all organizations use such a procedure!
Job advertisements are placed	Depending on the job, the urgency and the budget available, advertisements will be placed in appropriate newspapers, professional journals, job centres etc. You might be horrified to learn of the cost of such press advertising. Alternatively, the company might subcontract the whole recruitment process to recruitment

(Contd)

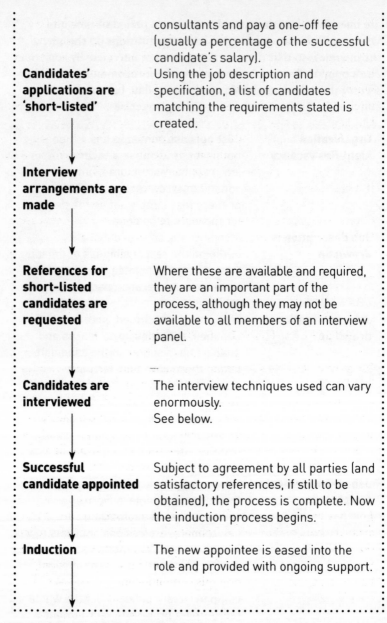

Candidates' applications are 'short-listed'

consultants and pay a one-off fee (usually a percentage of the successful candidate's salary).
Using the job description and specification, a list of candidates matching the requirements stated is created.

Interview arrangements are made

References for short-listed candidates are requested

Where these are available and required, they are an important part of the process, although they may not be available to all members of an interview panel.

Candidates are interviewed

The interview techniques used can vary enormously.
See below.

Successful candidate appointed

Subject to agreement by all parties (and satisfactory references, if still to be obtained), the process is complete. Now the induction process begins.

Induction

The new appointee is eased into the role and provided with ongoing support.

Figure 23 Stages of the job application/recruitment process.

In order to reach the interview it is likely that you will be asked to complete some or all of the following: an application form, curriculum vitae (CV) and a letter of application. Each of these is dealt with in more detail in 'Taking it Further' (pp. 176–86) where plenty of examples and tips are given. The same applies to interview technique (pp. 186–9). The important point to remember is that at each stage of the process you are marketing yourself. Your letter of request for the application details and forms will start your file (because organizations are always interested to assess the number of requests which are converted into applications). If it is scrappy it is not going to create a good impression.

Given the range of options available, let's see how our three case studies are progressing.

_____

Case studies

JANE PREPARES TO TAKE THE PLUNGE

With the end of the summer term in sight, Jane has steadily been building up her client base and her order-book. She has plenty to keep her occupied during the six-week holiday period, but has also made a particular effort to seek information from the Head so that she can also build in planning for next term's work. Jane still has sufficient professionalism to ensure that her pupils and colleagues do not suffer because she is making alternative career arrangements.

Jane has spoken with her pension provider and has made arrangements to 'buy in' additional years and has also researched the personal pensions market for when she becomes self-employed. She has budgeted for this in her plans and knows that it would be short-sighted to overlook this commitment. As a believer in 'personal privatization', she does not wish to end up in the 'misery gap' when she finally finishes work.

Jane now feels ready to take the plunge in a year's time. She has started to draw up an action plan so that she can ensure that various strategies and arrangements are in place for when she leaves. She realizes that her timetabling experience in school has been helpful in creating this schedule.

FRANCIS MAKES PROGRESS

Francis has made some tentative enquiries about similar employment in the same sector or indeed about self-employment. He has ruled out the latter, feeling that he lacks the necessary qualities to make a success of this. There are some possibilities with other employers, but he has rapidly learnt that the working environment is similar in all financial institutions, and that many posts are currently fragile.

He has made a few applications for several internal posts at the regional head office and has got further than ever before in his applications. The prospect of a job at regional level appeals now as he is realizing those latent skills and strengths within. He is optimistic and enjoying life more than for a long time.

RAMISH CONTINUES ON HIS PATH

Ramish is making progress with his enquiries about setting up a private practice. He is currently seeking advice from his professional body which is supportive.

In his own time he is attending a brief marketing course at his local college and is drawing up a business plan. Things are going well and he is particularly pleased by the interest and support of his colleagues. Even one of the senior managers has dropped in to chat with him, expressing his admiration for the courageous way Ramish wants to implement his plans.

THINGS TO REMEMBER

We have considered:

▶ *Useful planning tools for making informed choices.*

▶ *Some helpful sources of support.*

▶ *The job application and interview process.*

▶ *Good practice for job applications and interviews.*

▶ *Knowing that the core elements of satisfying work include:*
  ▷ *identifying work with congruent values to your own*
  ▷ *finding work that suits your personality*
  ▷ *matching your developing skill-set to work, and*
  ▷ *creating and building opportunities to develop yourself.*

ACTION POINTS

▶ *How much development has there been with the opportunities you foresaw for yourself at the end of the last chapter?*

▶ *If this is too early, what deadline are you setting yourself to see some development?*

▶ *Devise a personal force field analysis to assist your planning.*

Driving forces

Restraining forces

My force field analysis

9

Action planning

In this chapter you will learn:
* *how to devise your own action plan*
* *how to review and evaluate action plans*
* *about what you have learnt about yourself!*

Devising an action plan

By this stage you should feel reasonably confident about what you
have discovered about yourself, your motivations, your aspirations
and where you are most likely to find fulfilling and rewarding
work.

However, it is very easy to let your enthusiasm and good intentions
drift. So you need a structure to help you keep focused and to
check whether you are achieving your objectives. This is where
an **action plan** comes in. You can, for example, use it to monitor
your plans, including your force field analysis. An action plan is
simply a plan of action – it's no more difficult than that. But, for an
action plan to work effectively, a useful mnemonic to remember is
SMART. An action plan should be:

▶ *Specific*
▶ *Measurable*
▶ *Achievable*
▶ *Realistic*
▶ *Time-bound.*

Below you will find three action plans for you to complete, using the SMART scheme. The action plans cover short-term aims (i.e. next six months), medium-term aims (i.e. six months to two years' time) and long-term aims (i.e. two years or longer).

1 Short-term aims (the next six months)

Things I want to change in the workplace

▶ **S**

▶ **M**

▶ **A**

▶ **R**

▶ **T**

Things I want to change about my lifestyle

▶ **S**

▶ M

▶ A

▶ R

▶ T

Things I want to change about me

▶ S

▶ M

▶ A

(Contd)

▶ R

▶ T

My sources of support:

▶ *Financial*

▶ *People*

How will I know if I have achieved my aims?

2 Medium-term aims (six months to two years)

Things I want to change in the workplace

▶ **S**

▶ M

▶ A

▶ R

▶ T

Things I want to change about my lifestyle

▶ S

▶ M

▶ A

(Contd)

▶ **R**

▶ **T**

Things I want to change about me

▶ **S**

▶ **M**

▶ **A**

▶ **R**

▶ **T**

My sources of support:

▶ *Financial*

▶ *People*

How will I know if I have achieved my aims?

3 Long-term aims (two years or longer)

Things I want to change in the workplace

▶ **S**

▶ **M**

▶ **A**

(Contd)

▶ **R**

▶ **T**

Things I want to change about my lifestyle

▶ **S**

▶ **M**

▶ **A**

▶ **R**

▶ **T**

Things I want to change about me

▶ **S**

▶ **M**

▶ **A**

▶ **R**

▶ **T**

My sources of support:

▶ *Financial*

▶ *People*

(Contd)

How will I know if I have achieved my aims?

Filling in these boxes may have seemed quite time consuming but it's important to be able to have some support in your plans. You have identified these sources of support and also some of your milestones, as well as indicating whether there are specific changes you want to achieve over time. Such planning will help clarify your ideas and your plans by getting you to focus clearly. It won't necessarily prevent mistakes – but a mistake is only a mistake if you don't learn from it. We all learn from these and for many years, 3M's most successful product (the Post-It® note) has been the result of a mistake – an adhesive which did not work as intended.

Keeping yourself in mind

You should be at the forefront of your thoughts in your planning. This is not selfishness – you have already identified those others who are dear to you and for whom you have responsibilities. You are already taking their needs into account in your planning. Furthermore, by being pro-active, you are taking much more control of the situation than just waiting for things to happen to you (and to them) over which you have no control.

However, it is easy to get dissuaded from your plans and to let time catch up. To help overcome this you will find it beneficial to keep a clear note of:

- *your intentions*
- *your plans*
- *your targets.*

Prioritizing activities

If you want to make the most out of life, you will be seeking new opportunities and challenges. Sometimes, there may be too many to choose from and so you will have to consider 'Which of these should I pick?' You may need to remind yourself of your core purpose, of what you really want to achieve.

For example, if Jane (still remaining as a primary school teacher) were to join one of the school working parties, which of the following might be of greatest help to her in her plans (assuming that her contributions were of equal value to the school)?

- *marketing*
- *assessment*
- *boys' sports*
- *school uniform.*

Marketing would clearly seem to be the obvious choice – it could teach Jane a great deal about the fundamentals of marketing her own wares also (albeit in a different context). She would certainly gain far more than from the others whose values and aims would not be 'congruent' with her own. With those, she could well discover that she was putting in a lot of additional effort to gain little knowledge and few skills which were transferable to her own situation. Yet, by volunteering for the marketing working-party, Jane would not only be able to gain directly and relevantly herself, but also to contribute her growing expertise and maintain goodwill. As indicated earlier, employability skills cut both ways and will never be lost on your current employer.

Talking yourself up

Making decisions to change fundamental aspects of your life or
to retain the same position but with a different perspective on life
can be hard. The value of having someone with whom you can talk
openly has already been stressed. Vital also is the quality of feedback
which you get from others. But you also need feedback from
yourself, to motivate you by recognizing what you have achieved
and how you can meet your targets. The following tips can help:

- *Identify your continuing achievements.*
- *Quantify the progress you have made.*
- *Reflect on what you have done and ask yourself: 'In order to
  carry out that task, what skills and abilities do I have?' Likewise,
  ask yourself: 'What do I need to be good at to do this?'*
- *List your skills and abilities!*

Take the time to talk to yourself. This could be whilst sitting
at traffic lights, on the train home or as you go to sleep. You
can do so silently if necessary! Say 'Well done', give yourself a
metaphorical pat on the back and take pride in what you have
done. In other words, as the saying goes, 'Make an appointment
with yourself'.

Keeping on track

You might like to think about the decisions you have made for
your journey as being like planning a journey by hot-air balloon
(see Figure 24). It's your idea – your release from what you are
doing now. You are the force to provide lift-off – but you have to
show that it's more than hot air.

It's you who is doing the planning for the journey – you are
planning your route, your supplies, the distance to travel and the

duration of the journey. Is it a long-distance trip? Are you in it for the duration? Do you want to see what the journey is like before you commit yourself to a long-haul? You are also considering the altitude you wish to travel at – how high do you want to go?

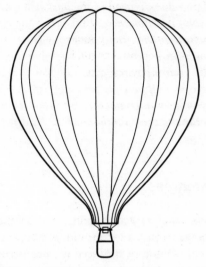

Figure 24 What do you need for a successful hot-air balloon journey?

You also need to check whilst you are preparing your balloon that it is securely tethered to the ground – that there is security. But at the point of lift-off you need to cut those ties and gradually jettison that ballast. What is your plan for this?

During the planning you'll need to take into account the expert opinion of others about the equipment and supplies you will need. You'll need to budget to determine the likely cost (in financial and other terms). You would be wise to get a meteorologist's forecast for the conditions you are likely to encounter. You will also need the forecast during the journey so that you can avoid extreme conditions or turbulence. You will need to consider who you are taking along for the ride and what contribution they are going to make to the journey – and what they are going to gain from it.

You will need to keep in touch with someone whose feet are firmly on the ground – your ground crew or observer.

In summary:

- ▶ *What and who do you need in the basket?*
- ▶ *What and who is providing the lift-off?*
- ▶ *Who and what are the ties to the ground?*
- ▶ *Who will be your expert?*
- ▶ *Who will be your meteorologist?*
- ▶ *Who, if anyone, will be your passenger/s?*
- ▶ *Who will you keep in contact with to report on progress?*
- ▶ *What might make the balloon crash or fly off-course?*

Evaluating progress

Such motivational small-talk as described in 'Talking yourself up' may not always be easy and you should not get carried away with false praise. It should be balanced with constructive criticism of where you may feel you still need to improve, such as in the example below:

> That meeting was pretty awful, wasn't it? I rushed through my point of view, didn't do my homework on how Jones would react, and didn't have a clear answer to the problem with deadlines. How stupid! Still, I know how to handle that in future: check out the likely impact on Jones' department, take my time with the proposals (maybe prepare a PowerPoint presentation) and check all my facts in advance.

Things will not always go well and you need to have the courage to evaluate your own progression and to improve any shortcomings in your own expectations of yourself.

Evaluating by considering key points

▶ *Keep your targets in mind and review them regularly.*
▶ *Praise your achievements.*
▶ *Evaluate where and why some things have not gone so well.*
▶ *Identify the causes of this.*
▶ *Try to remedy the situation by setting achievable targets.*
▶ *If necessary, be realistic and revise your targets or time-scales.*

Case studies

JANE

Having set herself a target of a year's time before leaving, Jane has established some key targets and deadlines as part of her action plan. She is now six months into this and everything seems to be going well.

She knows that initially things will be tough and that she will need extra financial support. She has approached a supply teaching agency and enrolled on their books. She knows that the pay will be less than she currently gets, that it can be hard going into a new school at very short notice and that supply teachers often get a raw deal. Nevertheless, it's a tremendous lifeline to her. However, she also knows that she must not become complacent about this and that if her new career is really going to work she has to be self-supporting as quickly as possible. She has given herself two years in her long-term action plan to do this.

FRANCIS

Francis has heard good news about his application for a post in the Regional Office. After a series of interviews, he has been appointed to a post which has an emphasis on systems and structures. It will be his responsibility to explain these and implement them with colleagues. Francis feels that he is well-suited to this post – it encompasses some of the aspects about which he feels strongly but is also going to make use of his new-found skills in explaining complexities in simple language. It is a real challenge to Francis but one he relishes and feels ready for.

Clearly, Francis has decided to stay with the same employer. He has done so after considerable soul-searching and research into alternatives. He stays, having learnt a great deal more about himself and the organization and with a much greater sense of self-confidence. Some of his personal values have changed, he has become more honest with himself and, whilst he looks forward to his new post with enthusiasm, he feels more confident about his own future employability skills. He knows that he must keep his own personal agenda to the fore and not slip back into becoming merely a 'company man'.

RAMISH

Ramish has decided to take up the opportunity to go into practice with a private-practice osteopath who is planning to retire in the next two years. The Health Authority has agreed to his request to keep him on the books for the next six months in a part-time capacity to cover a colleague's maternity leave. He has also negotiated a contract that it will buy-in his services privately in order to reduce waiting lists. This will be at a lower rate than he could charge patients directly but it is an assured income and gives some welcome stability over the next two years.

Ramish's principal concern and where he devotes much of his planning is in building up a practice which can offer a variety of complementary medical services. The premises are right, the owner sees it as a way of reducing his overheads, personal involvement other than as a 'sleeping partner' and making the practice more saleable, particularly as Ramish will be putting in his own time and expertise. Ramish has taken clear legal and financial advice on this so that it works in his favour. He is delighted with the way things are working out. Ramish feels a sense of control over his destiny once more and that he is able to live out his values again.

THINGS TO REMEMBER

In this final chapter we have considered:

▶ *The importance of devising realistic action plans.*

▶ *The importance of evaluating and reviewing action plans.*

▶ *The importance of talking yourself up.*

▶ *The importance of using others to stay motivated and finally...*

▶ *The importance of you.*

ACTION POINTS

The action points below are *your* future!

Postscript

At times things will be difficult. You may feel alone, you may feel that your 'sad captains' have deserted you, and that you alone are responsible for the decisions you make. But ultimately, you will have the satisfaction of knowing that you have taken more control of your life, and that whatever decisions you make, they are ones with which you can live. This feeling is eloquently expressed in the poem *The Road Not Taken* by the American poet Robert Frost:

> **Two roads diverged in a wood, and I –**
> **I took the one less travelled by,**
> **and that has made all the difference.**

From *The Poetry of Robert Frost*,
edited by Edward Connery Latham (Jonathan Cape)

You too, like Jane and Ramish, may reject the well-worn path, the apparently clearly laid-out route, and the route taken by the crowd. Or, like Francis, you may decide that as you have already started on a particular well-travelled path you are committed to it. You have tended and nurtured it. It is too late to turn back or to take a side-track, and for you, the benefits of the well-worn path outweigh the risks of losing your way, of unknown obstacles and a lack of clear sign-posting on the less-travelled path.

Whichever decision you make, you know that it is based on what you now understand about yourself and where you want to go. Whichever road you take – well-worn or less travelled by – enjoy it.

Taking it further

Applying for a job

COMPLETING THE APPLICATION FORM

Apart from very small organizations, most employers have a job application form which allows them to ask the same questions in the same sequence to all candidates. Clearly this has advantages in terms of fairness and consistency and certainly helps employers meet EU employment legislation. Unfortunately, not all application forms take into account the needs of the applicant. Some forms may be very cramped, have lots of space allocated for internal personnel department use, be repetitious or not allow the candidates to expand on key areas such as past experience. On one supermarket group's application form the most important element seemed to be applicant's hat size – hardly important until the induction process!

Nevertheless, making a good impact on the written application form is clearly important as it is the first (and perhaps only) set of information seen by the potential employer. Below are some tips for filling in the application form.

Tips for completing an application form:
▶ *Match up your experience to the qualities and experience sought.*
▶ *Follow instructions such as 'Use black ink' or 'Use block capitals'.*
▶ *Don't leave gaps.*
▶ *Practise on a photocopy to maximize spacing and layout.*
▶ *Keep a copy for future reference.*

It is becoming increasingly common with some large organizations to scan through applications electronically for key words. If the job advertisement has demanded 'experience of using Access databases', 'ability to demonstrate initiative', 'educated to A level/ NVQ Level 3 standard' or 'minimum of five years' experience in fast-moving consumer goods', the scanning process will pick up these terms and reject any other applications, no matter how good they may be otherwise. So always ensure that you use the key terms demanded.

In particular, try to show that you are a suitable candidate for the post in question. If you have been completing a number of application forms for different posts, it can be difficult to retain your enthusiasm for each separate job. Unfortunately, such lack of enthusiasm and matching of your own skills and experience to the post can show through to the employer – so you have to stick at it.

Lots of jobs are not actually advertised. You may be asked whether your application can be kept on file. If, generally, you have made a good impression but were not quite appropriate for the post in question, you may be alerted to other forthcoming vacancies. So, it's always worth making a good application.

DEVISING YOUR CURRICULUM VITAE

A **curriculum vitae** (CV) is usually demanded for most jobs, particularly for those where there is no application form. Small companies may rely more on a CV than anything else – they are simply too small to have a personnel department infrastructure and it is not cost-effective to devise their own application forms.

Your CV sets out in a structured manner your past relevant history (*curriculum vitae* is the Latin for 'outline of your life'). There are several different ways of setting out a CV and you might want to look at one of many books on devising a CV for a range of examples. However, here are some tips.

▶ *A CV must always be typed/word-processed.*

Insight

A typed CV looks more 'professional', you can get more on the page than with hand-writing and it allows you to easily arrange information under the different headings. You can update the content easily, saving you considerable time and effort.

▶ *Devise different CVs for different types of employment so that you can stress different skills and experiences.*

Insight

Your CVs may be markedly different in content and certainly you should not lie in any part of the application or interview process. However, the job-specific skills, qualities and experiences sought in different jobs may vary considerably. Naturally, the generic soft skills and key transferable skills sought will be similar across all employment sectors. Those aspects will not change. Having slightly different CVs will allow you to stress different aspects and give you flexibility. For example, if you are an engineer, possible posts may vary in the amount of engineering-specific, project-management or people-management responsibilities. The same CV may not stress sufficiently your experience in the areas sought. Likewise, the administrative skills sought in a hospital environment may be different from in a department store. Whilst some skills and qualities will remain generic (e.g. well-organized, efficient, familiar with appropriate IT packages), it may be that a hospital employer is seeking staff with an awareness of the implications of litigation if certain health-care protocols are not followed.

▶ *Present your employment history in reverse chronological order (unless you have very limited employment history).*

Insight

Reverse chronological order is better because it allows a prospective employer to see at a glance what you are doing now – how you got there is a less important concern when scanning through the whole CV.

▶ *Ensure that your CV looks attractively set out but avoid coloured paper, bows or other distractions.*

Insight

Presentation is all-important. Use good quality white paper (e.g. a 100 gsm brand like 'Conqueror' or 'Heritage'). Do not use coloured paper (which is difficult for the employer to photocopy) and avoid the technique used by some agencies of tying a bow around it. A simple, understated appearance creates a much more positive impression. Remember that you cannot make a poor CV look good just by using expensive, heavyweight coloured paper. Save the money for postage!

▶ *Limit the length of your CV to a maximum of two single-sided sheets of A4 paper.*

Insight

Try to restrict it to one side of A4 paper if you have only several years' experience or to a maximum of two sides even for someone currently in a senior position. Any longer only suggests that you do not have editing and prioritizing skills!

▶ *Use the CV to emphasize experiences/qualities which it may be difficult to explain in an application form.*

Insight

Depending on what other documentation you may be submitting (e.g. a CV and letter only), you can use the CV to highlight aspects which it may be more difficult to stress in another format. For example, you can see the range of training undertaken by Tina (p. 181) which would be rather cumbersome to express in a letter.

Several samples follow (pp. 181–3). Figure 25 has fairly standard headings, whilst Figure 26 incorporates a summary of the candidate's own estimation of their qualities. Either you like the latter approach (in which no one ever portrays a negative impression of themselves) or you do not. The same applies to employers, so you may feel safer erring towards the former layout and to reserve the qualities for the letter of application (see below).

Additionally, there is now a European standard 'Europass CV' which can be used to incorporate linguistic abilities and is particularly useful for those aiming to work in other EU member states.

WRITING YOUR LETTER OF APPLICATION

Some organizations request a **letter of application**. It is always beneficial to include one, even as a covering letter. The letter gives you the opportunity to expand upon and to emphasize points which you may be able to refer to only briefly in your CV or application form. It allows you to sell yourself as an individual. A good letter can be a powerful weapon – a poor letter will send your application to the bin.

	Curriculum Vitae
Name:	Tina Gaynor Smith
Address:	64 Helmsley Heights, Digbarton, Birmingham B29 7AZ
	Tina34@hotshotmail.com
	Home tel.: 0121 473 9375
	Work: 01678 455934 ext 428
	Mobile: 07455 928366
Nationality:	British
Education:	Chingley Comprehensive School, Chingley 1993–2000
	Digbarton College, 2000–2002
	Trimdon College of HE, 2005–2007 (p/t)
Qualifications:	8 GCSE passes (Grades C) including English Language and Maths, 2000
	BTEC National Diploma, Business & Finance (Distinction), 2002
	HNC, Business and Finance (Merit), 2008
Experience:	Clerical Assistant, Housing Section, Wheely Council 2002–2004

	Senior Clerical Officer, Kidglove Borough Council 2004–2007
	Executive Officer, Kidglove Borough Council 2007
Current principal responsibilities:	Administration of council tax across borough
	(including billing, council tax arrears, appeals, liaison with property services department).
	Team leader of 8 staff.
	Member of working party on new IT systems management.
Recent training:	Familiarization with new version of Microsoft Office (2007)
	Appraisal skills training (2009)
	Regular updates on housing law and public sector finance (ongoing)
	Training the trainer: 3-day course in planning, organizing, delivering and evaluating in-house training events (Summer 2010)

Figure 25 Sample curriculum vitae 1.

Curriculum Vitae

Tina Smith: a lively, outgoing high-achiever driven by results. A fast-learning team-leader with strong communication, interpersonal and organizational skills who thrives amid challenge and remains calm under pressure. Proven expertise in Customer Care and IT.

Name:	Tina Gaynor Smith
Address:	64 Helmsley Heights, Digbarton, Birmingham B29 7AZ
	Tina34@hotshotmail.com
	Tel: Home: 0121 473 9375
	Work: 01678 455934 ext 428
	Mobile: 07455 928366
Nationality:	British

(Contd)

Education: Chingley Comprehensive School, Chingley
                  1993–2000
                  Digbarton College, 2000–2002 (f/t)
                  Trimdon College of HE, 2005–2007 (p/t)
Qualifications: 8 GCSE passes (Grades C) including English
                  Language and Maths, 2000
                  BTEC National Diploma, Business & Finance
                  (Distinction), 2002
                  HNC, Business and Finance (Merit), 2008

Experience:

Clerical Assistant, Housing Section, Wheely Council 2002–2004
    Assisted in the administration of department, undertaking a
    wide range of tasks.
    Achieved the Council's 'Clerical employee of month' on five
    separate occasions.
    Oversaw the creation and administration of a range of
    tenant liaison activities during housing stock transfer.

Senior Clerical Officer, Kidglove Borough Council 2004–2007
    Assisted in organization of work schedules and work-loads
    for administrative staff.
    Implemented tailoring of new commercial software package
    for council – an estimated cost-saving of £38,000.
    Provided regular software training sessions for staff.
    Responsibility for servicing key departmental committees
    and council committees.

Executive Officer, Kidglove Borough Council 2007
    Administration of council tax across borough (including
    billing, arrears, appeals and liaison with property services
    department).
    Responsibility for a team of 8 staff.
    Established support systems for council tax enquiries:
    helpline, website, road-shows.
    Key involvement in preparing department for gaining
    Investors in People status throughout 2007. Award granted,
    Autumn 2009 with commendation to my department.

> Delegated responsibility within Council for staff training in a range of software packages and Customer Care.
>
> Recent training: Familiarization with new version of Microsoft Office (2007).
> Appraisal skills training (2009).
> Regular updates on housing law and public sector finance (ongoing).
> Training the trainer: 3-day course in planning, organizing, delivering and evaluating in-house training events (Summer 2010).

Figure 26 Sample curriculum vitae 2.

Ensure that you do your background research on the employer so that you can tailor your letter to this organization and this job. A bland, neutral letter does not impress and there are a variety of sources of information to find out about the employer, for example:

▶ *organization/company website*
▶ *national/local newspaper.*

If it's a local employer you can check out:

▶ *local library*
▶ *local newspaper (or the paper's website for less recent news).*

Tips for writing a letter of application

▶ *Note whether the instructions say the letter should be typed or handwritten – if you have a choice, base that decision on the quality of your handwriting.*
▶ *Use plain white A4 paper.*
▶ *Present yourself in a positive and confident light.*
▶ *Don't refer to your current (or previous) employer in a negative way.*
▶ *Take care with spelling, punctuation and phrasing.*
▶ *Use the appropriate ending depending on whether you know the name of the individual you are writing to. (If a given name, end* Yours sincerely, *if a title* Yours faithfully.)

Letters should always be to the point and not ramble. However, they do allow you to mesh what you want to say about yourself with the qualities and experience the post seeks. Do not play all your cards in your letter – you need to keep some detail back for interview, otherwise the interviewers may feel that there is no greater depth to you than was seen on paper.

Figure 27 is a sample of a brief covering letter. As a covering letter, there is no need for any further detail – the other documentation requested will provide this.

However, if your letter is part of the selling process, then it needs to be a *full letter*, outlining:

▶ *why you feel you are suited to the post*
▶ *cross-referring to your CV and application form*
▶ *enthusing about the opportunities provided by the post.*

In this case, Tina's letter might look like Figure 28.

64 Helmsley Heights
Digbarton
Birmingham B29 7AZ
4 November 2010

Ms Sonia Bramhall
Head of Personnel
Trimdon County Borough Council
Sunnyside Enterprise Park
Trimdon TR2 5NS

Dear Ms Bramhall

Application for post of Senior Executive Officer, Housing Department Ref 07/H12

Please find attached a copy of my application form and CV for the above post.

I look forward to hearing from you in due course and to attending an interview if you shortlist me.

Yours sincerely

Tina Smith
Tina Smith

Figure 27 Sample of a brief covering letter.

64 Helmsley Heights
Digbarton
Birmingham B29 7AZ
4 November 2010

Ms Sonia Bramhall
Head of Personnel
Trimdon County Borough Council
Sunnyside Enterprise Park
Trimdon TR2 5NS

Dear Ms Bramhall

<u>Application for post of Senior Executive Officer, Housing
Department Ref 09/H12</u>

Please find attached a copy of my application form and CV for the above post. I am very enthusiastic about the above opportunity and would like to outline the reasons for my application.

As you will note from my CV I have considerable experience in the field of local government and within the housing sector generally. My experience includes a number of key areas which are integral to this post.

I have up-to-date familiarity with housing legislation and the rights of the tenant, having undertaken specific training in this field.

(Contd)

My work has given me an overview of systems management and I was part of a working party in tailoring a commercial software package for use in the local authority. Its implementation has been very successful, both from the authority's point of view and the tenants.

I have developed a high level of interpersonal skills through building teams and in persuading people to achieve and exceed their own targets. I played a key role in the success of my department in achieving Investors in People status, and in liaising with members of the public by setting up support mechanisms.

At Wheely District Council I assisted with the transfer of the housing stock from the Council to the Vale Housing Association. This involved liaison with tenants through: devising questionnaires, drafting information packs and arranging focus groups and meetings.

I look forward to hearing from you in due course and to attending an interview should you shortlist me.

Yours sincerely

Tina Smith
Tina Smith

Figure 28 Sample of extended covering letter.

Job interviews

PREPARING FOR YOUR INTERVIEW

Of course, the aim of a good application is to gain an interview. When called to interview, treat the invitation accordingly – it shows that you have impressed on paper. Now they want to learn more about you.

Before the interview

▶ *Consider the types of question you might be asked – both general and job-specific.*
▶ *Consider your strengths for the post.*
▶ *Consider your wider strengths as an employee of the organization.*
▶ *Identify some 'allowable' weakness.*
▶ *Be positive about your chances.*

Of course, you will have considered and prepared for many of these stages as a result of reading this book. For example, if the vacancy is in your existing employment sector, your PEST should be accurate (as long as it was done recently!). It should also assist you with identifying some of the questions which you might be asked. For example, Francis might be asked questions about the impact of changing customer expectations on the financial services sector. This preparation itself will place you in a stronger position for an interview. However, there are additional areas you should also consider.

Re-read your application

Particularly if you have several applications for different posts, you'll need to refresh your mind for exactly what you said for this post. Nothing irritates an interviewer more than a candidate thinking about or referring to another employer or post. Ensure that you are familiar with the application you made and how you identified that your background skills, knowledge and experience suited you to the post.

Carry out some further research on the organization and the job

It makes sense to research data as much as you can as previously stated.

Arrive on time

Check out likely times for travel – and then allow some more. The last thing you want is to arrive breathlessly because you missed a connection or couldn't find a parking space.

Dress appropriately

There is no absolute code here but it generally pays to err on the side of formality and to dress smartly, but comfortably. Collars which are too tight and skirts which need constant adjustment should be avoided. Employers will generally expect you to have made an effort in your appearance, showing that you are taking the opportunity seriously. Beyond that, people's taste in clothes is so varied that specific advice is counter-productive.

DURING THE INTERVIEW

Differentiate between closed and open questions

A skilled interviewer knows the right sort of questions to ask and when. Closed questions usually seek simple 'yes' or 'no' answers. They close the conversation down but may have a place in clarifying an issue or just as an ice-breaker. For example, 'Did you find our office OK?' is simply an ice-breaker and is not assessing your map-reading skills.

Most interview questions will be open-ended (i.e. encouraging you to open up the conversation). Many of the questions you have encountered in this book have been open questions to encourage you to think about your own situation. An interviewer can only assess the effectiveness of the interviewee on the quality of the answers given, so appropriate questions are crucial. If you find that you are only being asked limited questions, don't be afraid to take the initiative. For example:

Interviewer: Have you had people-management experience? (A poor simple yes/no question which is not very illuminating.)

Interviewee: Yes. For the last two years in my current post I have been responsible for a team of ... and for the previous three years of my last post I had a team of ... people. Etc, etc.

This will allow you far more scope to answer more fully and to give specific examples of experiences and also of identifying problems and how you overcame them.

Make eye contact with all the interviewers

Often you will be interviewed by a panel of interviewers – each with an area of responsibility or expertise both in the workplace and for the interview. One may be focusing on job-specific issues, one on interpersonal skills and another on management issues. It is important that all interviewers feel that they are involved in your answers so make sure that you look at each of them not just the questioner.

It is often said that in Western society conversations:

▶ *the listener looks at the speaker for 75% of the time*
▶ *the speaker looks at the listener for 40% of the time*
▶ *both look at each other for 30% of the time*
▶ *the length of each mutual glance is only 1.5 seconds.*

Any direct eye-to-eye contact over a few seconds may be considered a transfixing stare and is potentially threatening. So keep it brief and cast your eyes around other interviewers.

Answer questions directly – don't waffle

Your ability to answer questions is, of course, being assessed. Listen to the question carefully, identify and prioritize your response – the human mind can do this very quickly.

Have a question ready to show that you have prepared and are taking an interest in the organization

All interviews are a two-way process and you are perfectly entitled to ask questions during an interview. Many organizations include as part of the interview schedule a tour around the facilities and it is here that it may be appropriate to ask certain questions, as you view plant, buildings, staff or systems. Often, these will be job-specific questions or general ones about the employer, rather than ones which apply to your own situation if you were offered the job. However, within the interview itself, there should always be an opportunity for you to ask questions – if there isn't, take the initiative and ask them anyway. Do make sure that you are absolutely clear about terms and conditions of work (including pay) before accepting a post – you should not feel awkward about seeking such clarification.

At the same time, try to make sure that any questions you ask are not just to do with pay or holiday entitlement, or you will come over simply as a one-dimensional person interested only in taking from the employer. Remember that an effective way of asking a question is to make a statement first, showing that you have an understanding of certain aspects of operation. For example:

▶ *'I note that you introduced continuous feed un-loaders twelve months ago. Did this cause any problems with operators used to a two-shift system?'*
▶ *'You explained that there was a matrix system for monitoring quality – that senior managers had responsibility both for a functional area and a staff-grouping. Can you explain in more detail exactly how this works so that there are no gaps or overlap in accountability.'*

If you are interviewed on the same day as other candidates, keep your own counsel when you are alone with them – don't give away your own strengths
For many posts in the public sector, interviewees are interviewed the same day and it is highly likely that you will be with others at times, waiting for the next stage of the proceedings. Given that interviews are competitive, it is clearly not in your interest to give any other interviewee information about your own weaknesses which might, somehow or other, be used as ammunition. Keep the conversation bland – it is fine to keep each other's spirits up by talking about the weather, holidays or sports matches.

Smile but don't grin
Remember that you are going to be working as part of a team so one of the aspects being assessed is your range of interpersonal skills, your ability to get on with other people and your reaction under pressure. All interviewers recognize that an interview can be stressful for interviewees – indeed, it is stressful for interviewers also. Smiling conveys confidence, enthusiasm, eagerness, a sense of

humour and even an indication that you do not take yourself too seriously. By contrast, fixed grins can indicate nerves and even, in some circumstances, aggression.

Sound positive about the job prospects
For obvious reasons the interviewers need to be convinced that you are positive about the current post and possible progression.

Keep your body language positive
Flopping back, slumped in your chair, whilst at the same time talking about your enthusiasm simply conveys a mixed message. Be upright without starchiness and use restrained hand and arm gestures to reinforce your meaning.

As with the section on job applications, take the opportunity to consult a book dealing with this topic. See the Further reading on pp. 198–9 for details.

Useful addresses

CAREERS ORGANIZATIONS

England: www.connexions.gov.uk
Although this is principally aimed at school and college age learners, there are some useful links to careers sites for adults.

Wales: www.careerswales.com/adult/default.asp?conid=adults
Although the direct link to information for adults is a bit of a mouthful, this is a useful site featuring a 'CV Wizard'.

Scotland: www.careers-scotland.org.uk
As with Wales, this also includes a 'CV builder'.

Northern Ireland: www.careersserviceni.com/Cultures/en-GB/
As with the other devolved nations of the UK, this site has a 'CV Generator'. Although principally aimed at younger people, there

are links and downloads for career changers and those wishing to establish their own business.

Additionally, there are many private careers advice organizations, which you can check out locally.

ORGANIZATIONS OFFERING INFORMATION ON FINANCING FURTHER/HIGHER EDUCATION OPPORTUNITIES

Career Development Loans, Freepost, Newcastle-upon-Tyne X NE85 1BR or phone 0800 585505. www.lifelonglearning. co.uk/cdl/
Offers deferred repayment loans from £300 to £8,000 to provide individuals with help to fund vocational education or learning. Arranged through certain High Street banks but all information coordinated by DirectGov.uk at above address.

The Student Loans Company Ltd, 100 Bothwell Street, Glasgow G2 7JD. Tel 0870 240 6298 Website: www.slc.co.uk
Administers loans for accredited courses in higher education.

Student Awards Agency for Scotland, Gyleview House, 3 Redheughs Rigg, South Gyle, Edinburgh EH12 9HH. Tel 0845 111 1711 www.student-support-saas.gov.uk Currently student awards in Scotland are coordinated through this agency, whereas in England and Wales it is through the student's local council.

ORGANIZATIONS OFFERING INFORMATION OR ADVICE ON FURTHER TRAINING OR EDUCATION

DIUS Lifelong Learning website: www.lifelonglearning.co.uk.
Provides a range of information on opportunities in lifelong learning across the UK and also information on Career Development Loans.

Learndirect. 0800 1-1 901 www.learndirect.co.uk.
Developed by the University for Industry (UfI) to offer advice on and contact with training providers across England, Wales and

Northern Ireland. Advice and courses are available in a variety of languages (e.g. Welsh, Urdu, Bengali, Somali). The freephone number connects you to your regional centre.

National Open College Network: www.nocn.org.uk
The UK's principal provider of accreditation for adult learning. It is not a learning provider itself, but you can check online the level of any OCN course in which you are interested.

Open College of the Arts, OCA, Freepost SF10678 Tel 0800 731 2116; Website: www.oca-uk.com
A community of artists, writers and designers committed to unleashing individuals' creative potential.

Universities & Colleges Admissions Service (UCAS), PO Box 28, Cheltenham, Glos GL52 3LZ. Tel 0871 468 0468; Website: www.ucas.ac.uk

Education providers specializing in adult learners
Your local FE college across the UK. Look in your local newspaper or telephone directory.

Workers' Educational Association (WEA) website: www.wea.org.uk
Founded in 1903, the WEA is the UK's largest voluntary provider of adult and community education.

Higher education providers specializing in adult learners
Extra-Mural Departments/Departments of Adult Continuing Education
See your local press and telephone directory (under universities) for details. Most universities have community education programmes.

Birkbeck College, University of London
Information unit: 020 7631 6692; Website: www.bbk.ac.uk; Email: admissions@admin.bbk.ac.uk
Offers over 100 degree evening programmes and over 1,000 short courses, certificates and diplomas throughout London area.

Open University, General Enquiry Service, PO Box 200, Milton
Keynes MK7 6YZ. Tel 0845 300 6090; Website: www.open.ac.uk
Globally renowned for high quality materials and courses.

Institutions specializing in residential higher education for adults

Coleg Harlech, Harlech, Gwynedd LL46 2PU. Tel 01766 781900.
Website: www.harlech.ac.uk
Amalgamated with WEA North Wales to offer HE Diplomas
and is tailored to providing courses for mature students without
traditional entry qualifications.

Ruskin College, Walton Street, Oxford OX1 2HE. Tel 01865
554331. Website: www.ruskin.ac.uk
Well-established institution with strong trade-union links, with
long heritage of providing for those not traditionally able to access
educational opportunities.

Distance-learning centres offering MBAs etc.

See newspaper advertisements, particularly in the *Guardian*
(Tuesday), the *Daily Telegraph* (Wednesday).

IT courses

European Computer Driving Licence (ECDL).
A qualification which has gained great success in Europe,
particularly in Scandinavia, where it has become a routinely sought
qualification by employers. Available at a variety of locations
across the UK, mostly FE colleges. For information, contact: ECDL
UK, The British Computer Society, 1 Sanford Street, Swindon,
Wiltshire SN1 1HJ. Tel 01793 417424
Website: www.ecdl.co.uk; Email: ecdlenq@hq.bcs.org.uk

Organizations offering management support and training

The Chartered Management Institute, Management House,
Cottingham Road, Corby, Northants NN17 1TT. Tel 01536 204222.
Email: enquiries@managers.org.uk

Organizations providing information, advice or support to business start-ups

- *England: Business Links www.businesslink.gov.uk*
- *Wales: Business Eye www.business-support-wales.gov.uk*
- *Scotland: Business Gateway www.bgateway.com*
- *Northern Ireland: Invest Northern Ireland www.investni.com*

The last three are under the responsibility of the devolved administrations.

The Regional Development Agency in England now has similarly devolved responsibility for regional business development.

Many people starting up a business will head for their nearest Enterprise Agency, which you can locate through the National Federation of Enterprise Agencies website at www.nfea.com. This has links to the UK agencies outside England also.

If you fall into one of the particular sectors below, there are specialist agencies to advise you:

- **16 to 30 year olds:** *Shell Livewire (www.shell-livewire.org) and Prince's Trust (www.princes-trust.org.uk)*
- **Over 50s:** *PRIME: The Prince's Trust for Mature Enterprise (www.primeinitiative.org.uk)*
- **Women Entrepreneurs:** *The Women's Business Development Agency (WBDA) (www.wbda.co.uk)*
- **Disadvantaged communities and for ethnic minority entrepreneurs:** *The Community Development Finance Association (CDFA) has offices around the UK (www.cdfa.org.uk)*

Organizations providing opportunities to offer skills to others and 'find oneself'

Camp America, 37a Queen's Gate, London SW7 5HR
Tel 0207 581 7377 Email: enquiries@campamerica.co.uk;
Website: www.campamerica.co.uk

Offers to suitable candidates up to nine weeks' summer experience as a youth leader in USA (supervising children in camps, sports training etc., free transatlantic flight, accommodation and meals).

Voluntary Services Overseas (VSO), 317 Putney Bridge Road, London SW15 2PN; Tel 020 8780 7200; Website: www.vso.org.uk Offers to suitable (graduate) candidates with specific skills placements in Third World/emerging countries. Particularly needs candidates with teaching, engineering and agricultural expertise and qualifications.

Organizations offering job/recruitment leads
- *Your local Jobcentre (see telephone directory).*
- *Your local newspaper/s (check which day/evening feature most entries for job vacancies).*
- *National newspapers (especially if you are geographically mobile). Particularly useful are the* Daily Telegraph, *the* Daily Mail, *the* Daily Express *or the* Guardian. *Note also that the* Daily Telegraph *has an Appointments Plus website (www.telegraph.co.uk) giving links to industry associations and to psychometric testing.*

Organizations offering group and individual support in employability skills
CATS Email: info@ashley-consult.co.uk; Website: www.ashley-consult.co.uk Run by the author of this book. Offers courses in employability skills and job application and interview technique.

Teleworking
TCA (The Telework, Telecottage and Telecentre Association). Europe's largest organization dedicated to the promotion of teleworking. Associated also with TCW (Telecottages Wales), STA (Scottish Teleworking Association) and TWI (Telework Ireland). Has an excellent website. Membership Helpline: 0800 616008; Fax 01453 836174; Website www.telework.org.uk; Email: enquiries@telework.org.uk

Useful websites

www.bbc.co.uk/wales/raiseyourgame
This site on the BBC Wales Sports website is designed to raise
self-awareness, self-belief and enthusiasm through six key strands:
inspiration, motivation, preparation, concentration, dedication
and commitment. It is 'hosted' by the athlete Colin Jackson and,
whilst many of the references are to sports personalities, there are
many unsung heroes in non-sporting fields also who have found
fulfilment through their passion for their various pursuits. The
website is constantly updated so there are lots of topical examples
of how sports people have inspired themselves and others. There
are brief example of good and poor CV styles. The website is part-
funded by the Welsh Assembly Government which is committed to
the lifelong learning agenda outlined in Chapter 1.

www.belbin.com
The website of the Belbin organization run by the psychologist
and author, R. Meredith Belbin, whose work on teams we looked
at in Chapter 6. It offers the opportunity for self-assessment
questionnaires on team-working strengths.

www.businessballs.com
Provides a range of free information and resources on management.
Many of these are 'self-management' tools.

www.channel4.com/health
Contains a summary of the *Whitehall II study* in Chapter 8 and
of the link between stress and heart problems. The full link (at the
time of writing) is at www.channel4.com/health/ microsites/0-9/
4health/stress/aas_heart.html.

http://europass.cedefop.eu.int/europass/home/vernav/Europasss+
Documents/Europass/Europass+CV/csp

This links to information about the Europass CV and the move to
recognize EU member state qualifications across Europe.

Further reading

The following publications deal in more detail with many of the
topics raised in this book.

Interviews: How to Succeed. Rod Ashley (Tynron Press, 1990).
Management Teams: Why They Succeed or Fail. R. Meredith
  Belbin (Heinemann, 1982).
Jobshift. William Bridges (Nicholas Brealey, 1995).
Q Learning: MOTIVATOR. Frances Coombes (Hodder Arnold,
  2003).
The Seven Habits of Highly Effective People. Stephen R. Covey
  (Simon & Schuster, 1989).
The New Unblocked Manager. Dave Francis and Mike Woodcock
  (Gower, 1996).
Understanding Organizations. Charles Handy (Penguin, 1993).
The Motivation to Work. F. Herzberg, B. Mausner and B.
  Snyderman (Wiley, 1959).
Transferable Personal Skills (2nd edn). David Hind and Rod Ashley
  (Business Education Publishers, 1994).
The Learning Age. HM Government Green Paper (HMSO,
  February 1998).
Improve Your People Skills. Peter Honey (Institute of Personnel
  Management, 1988).
Set Up a Successful Small Business. Vera Hughes and David Weller
  (Teach Yourself, 2010).
Guide to the Management Gurus. Carol Kennedy (Century
  Business, 1991).
*Succeed at Psychometric Testing: Practice Tests for Verbal
  Reasoning Advanced*. Jeremy Kourdi (Hodder Education, 2008).
Motivation and Personality. Abraham Maslow (Harper & Row,
  1970).
The Human Problems of an Industrial Civilization. Elton Mayo
  (Macmillan, 1933).
The Human Side of Enterprise. Douglas McGregor (McGraw-Hill,
  1960).

When Giants Learn to Dance. Rosabeth Moss Kanter (Routledge, 1994).

Succeed at Psychometric Testing: Practice Tests for Verbal Reasoning Intermediate. Simbo Nuga (Hodder Education, 2008).

Winning at Job Interviews. Igor S. Popovich (Teach Yourself, 2003).

Succeed at Psychometric Testing: Practice Tests for Critical Verbal Reasoning. Peter S. Rhodes (Hodder Education, 2008).

Succeed at Psychometric Testing: Practice Tests for Diagrammatic and Abstract Reasoning. Peter S. Rhodes (Hodder Education, 2008).

Succeed at Psychometric Testing: Practice Tests for Personality Testing. Peter S. Rhodes (Hodder Education, 2008).

Career Dynamics: Matching Individual and Organizational Needs. Edgar Schein (Addison-Wesley, 1978).

Succeed at Psychometric Testing: Practice Tests for Data Interpretation. Sally Vanson (Hodder Arnold, 2004).

Succeed at Psychometric Testing: Practice Tests for Numerical Reasoning Intermediate. Bernice Walmsley (Hodder Education, 2008).

Succeed at Psychometric Testing: Practice Tests for Numerical Reasoning Advanced. Bernice Walmsley (Hodder Education, 2008).

Glossary

Accreditation of Prior Learning (APL) Giving credit for previous learning and achievement which may have taken place. It is common in NVQ qualifications (see below) to enhance flexibility of learning and to save going over ground with which learner is familiar and competent. Sometimes known as:

Accreditation of Prior Experience and Learning (APEL) Similar to above but relevant experience is also credited. A *bona fide* concept when rigorously implemented but beware 'offshore' universities which will credit 'students' with degrees in return for a steep fee and mere claims of previous 'life experience'.

Annualized hours An employment contract in which staff are required to work an average number of hours to a set annual total, but there may be significant variation in hours at different times of the year – college lecturers work such a contract.

Blended learning A mixture of learning approaches to both maximize the potential of certain learning strategies (e.g. the internet) and to provide variety.

Contingency worker Employment or jobs being reliant upon demand. If demand dips and there are no other tasks for the worker, his/her employment ceases.

Curriculum Vitae Commonly abbreviated to CV, this literally means 'an outline of your life'. Frequently used as a standard means of listing previous experience and qualifications when applying for work.

Distance Learning (DL) Where learning takes place physically away from the education provider (e.g. correspondence courses, learning via the internet and some aspects of the Open University's provision). *See also* Flexible Learning and Open Learning.

Downshift To take lower status work (including perhaps self-employment) because the perceived benefits (e.g. autonomy and variety) outweigh the perceived losses (e.g. perceived status, company infrastructure etc.).

EDAP (Employee Development Assistance Programme) Employees are allocated by their employer a 'voucher' which entitles them to education (as opposed to job-specific training) at the employer's expense. Ford, for example, has such a scheme and encourages all employees to use it in the belief that a learning workforce is enquiring, seeks change and improvement and sets itself high standards.

Eleven-plus The examination formerly sat by most pupils in parts of Britain at age 11 in order to determine whether they attended a grammar school (20%) or a secondary-modern school (80%). This examination was abolished in most areas with the introduction of all-ability comprehensive schools.

Emotional intelligence A term devised by Daniel Goleman who considered that the classic definition of intelligence was too narrow and that the emotional qualities of individuals also played an important role in the application of intelligence in daily life. Goleman identifies key characteristics as: self-motivation, persistence, controlling impulse, delaying gratification, ability to regulate moods and to keep personal distress from inhibiting thinking; to empathize and to hope. See D. Goleman (1998), *Working With Emotional Intelligence*, New York: Bantam.

Employability Retaining your attractiveness to employers through updating the skills, qualities and attributes you can offer.

Flexible Learning The use of learning packages which can be used flexibly, e.g. within or away from a learning establishment, as a means of delivering a complete course or just part of it. *See also* Distance Learning and Open Learning.

Global economy Using the full potential of achieving economies of scale through sourcing materials, utilizing cheap labour and maximizing market penetration on a world-wide scale.

Job A social contract into which we enter with an employer to spend an agreed number of hours per week in his/her employment in exchange for a certain sum of money which allows us, within financial constraints, to spend in the way we wish to pursue a particular lifestyle.

Job-share Division of the roles and tasks in a single job between two people (usually equally) who also share the income and benefits associated with that job. This facility promotes flexibility and can ensure that people who have other commitments (e.g. single parents or part-time students) can also access the labour market.

Learning Age The name of the seminal Government Green Paper (February 1998) which emphasized the importance of developing skills and knowledge for both employability and personal fulfilment in the twenty-first century.

Learning credits A system to encourage ownership of learning whereby all learning and training is entered on a smart-card, thereby encouraging the learner to take advantage

of opportunities offered to build up a bank of recognized
knowledge, skills and qualifications.

Life-mapping Charting the most significant events in one's life
in order to understand the consequences of these events and
their impact upon the individual.

'Listening noises' Noises which give feedback to the speaker/s
to show that you are listening, e.g. 'Yes, I see...', 'OK,
right...' etc.

Mindset Mental attitude and set of values. Those with a
mindset which does not expect an employer to offer or
provide a lifelong job or who actively seek alternative means
of employment will develop greater employability skills than
those who have a passive expectation that the employer will
provide forever.

Misery gap The difference between actual pension income and
that needed to achieve a comfortable retirement.

Motivation theories Theories on the way in which people
are encouraged through positive motivation or coerced,
threatened and bullied through negative motivation to
improve their performance. The examples dealt with suggest
that individuals respond differently according to their needs
and personality.

Multiple intelligences Seven aspects of intelligence comprise
overall intelligence according to Howard Gardner. These are:
verbal, mathematical, spatial capacity, kinaesthetic, musical
and, importantly, personal intelligences (interpersonal skills
with others and intrapersonal skills of knowing oneself).
See H. Gardner (1993), *Frames of Mind*, London: Fontana.

National Curriculum The range and level of subjects which
children in British state schools study between the ages of
5 and 16.

National Health Service (NHS) The provision of state-funded medical and dental care in the UK.

Online learning Learning via the internet. Many course providers offer structured learning wholly (or at least partly) online. In the UK, Learndirect (0800 100900) is the government-backed gateway to learning online.

Open Learning (OL) Although there is no universally agreed definition of OL, the essential concept is of opening up new opportunities to learn. This can be done by, for example, enabling learners to study whatever, wherever and whenever they like and at a pace which suits them. *See also* Flexible Learning and Distance Learning.

Paramedic Someone engaged in a supporting medical role. E.g. Ramish in this book is an osteopath, supporting the work of orthopaedic surgeons, GPs and physiotherapists (the latter also being a paramedic discipline).

Personal privatization Increased personal responsibility for the costs of pension provision, welfare, educational and health costs.

PEST analysis Analysis of Political, Economic, Social trends and Technological changes which may affect a business – used in this book to consider impact of such changes on the individual's employability.

Portfolio A varied collection of work and responsibilities with a variety of clients or employers.

Production line Organization of production in a factory according to set procedures, sequences and costings. It has been traditional to employ people to carry out a single task only in the production.

Psychometric testing A series of written/graphical or other tests to determine an individual's psychological profile. Employers use such tests to screen out applicants before final selection. Alternatively, a number of psychological counselling services use such tests to advise individuals which careers, job sectors and types of employment they seem most suited or unsuited to. Check in broadsheet newspapers for addresses – mostly London – of such services.

Purchaser/provider Current National Health Service split whereby the Health Authorities (the purchasers) decide which medical, clinical and nursing and paramedic services to buy from hospital trusts, GP surgeries, dental practices, chiropodists etc. The latter are the providers of medical care.

Resiliency Having the strength of character to take the knocks and set-backs inevitable in today's working environment.

Self-actualization Achieving one's full potential. Maslow's concept is based on the premise in Robert Browning's poem, Andrea del Sarto:

**Ah, but a Man's reach should exceed his grasp,
Or what's a heaven for?**

SME A small or medium-sized enterprise. By definition, this is one employing between 50 and 300 people. In many areas of the UK (e.g. Wales and Northern Ireland), the greatest economic growth is in SMEs. For many people, this marks a shift in culture because they may have previously worked only for large organizations. For graduates in particular, the prospect of working for an SME has to be contemplated rather than for traditional corporate graduate-employers.

SWOT analysis An analysis of one's strengths, weaknesses, opportunities and threats. Frequently conducted by businesses in order to establish how they should develop, but can be applied to individual's circumstances also.

Technophobe Someone with a fear of technology. Often applies to people who do not like using or are reluctant to use computers. Colleges often provide courses on IT for the Terrified.

Techno-realist Someone with a realistic attitude to the opportunities, demands and implications of new (i.e. computer-related) technology. His/her views contrast with those of a technophile (who is obsessed with the technology and can see no dangers in it) and a techno-luddite (who resents anything to do with new technology).

Transferable skills Those skills which can be used in a variety of contexts whether in the workplace or in leisure, for example communication skills, keyboard skills, problem-solving skills and time-management skills.

Vendor-mindedness Being aware of how to sell your services, skills, knowledge, experience and attributes to a purchaser in return for a fee. From: *JOBSHIFT: How to Prosper in a Workplace Without Jobs* by William Bridges; published by Nicholas Brealey Publishing Ltd.

Work-life balance Retaining a healthy balance between work commitments and family or social life.

Index